Congregation Emunas Yisroel
4310 16th Avenue
Brooklyn, New York 11204

To Marsha Kaplon,

    Presented with deepest thanks for you having attended to our Rabbi in a friendly manner and with true dedication. We are grateful that your efforts were successful and we express our heartfelt good wishes for your continued success in all your endeavors.

Meir Lezer
646-645-5957

Meir Lezer
On behalf of the entire Congregation

Rabbi Moshe Wolfson - Rabbi

Board Members
R' Mordechai Finkelman , Mr. Yanky Friedman
Mr. Yanky Goldner , R' Shmuel Goldstein
R' Shmuel Dovid Hardt, Mr. Hertzy Hasenfeld
R' Shlomo Lezer

Wellsprings of FAITH

Wellsprings of FAITH

Perspectives
on the
Sources
of Emunah

Rabbi Moshe Wolfson

Translated and arranged by
Yehoshua Fieldsteel

FELDHEIM PUBLISHERS
JERUSALEM / NEW YORK

First published 2002

Copyright © 2002
by Yehoshua Fieldsteel

ISBN 1-58330-526-2

FELDHEIM PUBLISHERS
POB 35002 / Jerusalem, Israel

202 Airport Executive Park
Nanuet, NY 10954

www.feldheim.com

Printed in Israel

ב״ה

B"H
4 Kislev, 5762

To my dear friend Rabbi Yehoshua Fieldsteel *shlita*,
I read your manuscript, which is based on my *sefer*, *Emunas Itecha*, and it gave me great pleasure. Even though you have developed and broadened the ideas using the talents of a skillful writer and a style that is eloquent and scholarly, nevertheless, you have succeeded in maintaining the purity of the original ideas without any deviation from the intended meaning. The contents have been adorned with a crown of rhetorical beauty, and all this has been accomplished with discernment, intelligence, and taste. The result is a *sefer* that is very delightful and worthy of blessing. I offer my congratulations and thanks.

May Hashem help you to continue to enrich the literature of the holy Torah with additional delightful and useful *sefarim*. May you do so amidst joy, tranquillity and happiness, and may you be successful in all your endeavors.

With great friendship,
Rabbi Moshe Wolfson

RABBI I. J. WEISS

CHIEF RABBI

OF JERUSALEM

JERUSALEM, RECHOV YESHAYAHU 20

יצחק יעקב וייס

רב ואב"ד

לכל מקהלות האשכנזים פעיה"ק ירושלם תובב"א

מח"ס שו"ת מנחת יצחק

ירושלים, רחוב ישעיהו 20

בס"ד

ירושלים עה"ק ת"ו, יום ב' י"א לחודש הרחמים שמו"ת לפ"ק.

הן הובא לפני תכריך כתבים ונקובים בשם "אמונת עתיך" מכב"ת האי גברא רבא פה מפיק מרגליות המאור הגדול לממשלת התורה והיראה הרה"ג המפורסם בצדקתו רבי משה וואלפסאן שליט"א מנהיג דק"ק אמונת ישראל ומשגיח רוחני דישבה"ק תורה ודעת בברוקלין נ.י. וכבר נתפרסמו אמרותיו היקרים בדרוש ואגדה אשר בהם עולים כלולים ומשולבים יחדיו ספרי חסידות מוסר ומחשבה ומחקר, וכי ידיו של הרה"ג המחבר שליט"א רב לו להקים מרקחים ערבים ומתוקים המאירים ומשמחים את לבב המעיין, ואשר בלי ספק בכוחם לעורר את לב השומע לתורה לתשובה ולמעש"ט.

והנה המפורסמות א"צ ראי' כי הרה"ג המחבר שליט"א כל כוונתו בדבריו ובמעשיו היא לזכות את הרבים ולהעמידם בקרן אורה בזו זו תורה, וג' עמודים שעליהם העולם עומד, אשר על כן עתה כאשר נפשו איותה להוציא ויעש את כתביו לאור עולם, ולהביאם לבית הדפוס, אף ידי תיכון עמו לחזקו ולאמצו בדבר הזה, ולהגיד בזה בשער בת רבים שבח שבח המגיע לכתביו, וכאשר רבים שתו עד היום בצמא את דבריו שבע"פ, כן ודאי ישתו רבים רבים את דבריו שבכתב, ויתענגו ע"ד אמת.

ויהא רעוא שכשם שהדברים יצאו מלבו הטהור כן יכנסו ללבבות ישראל קדושים, לחזק ברכים כושלות, ולהשיב נפשות לעבודתו ית"ש, כחפץ לבבו הטהור של הרה"ג המחבר שליט"א, ובמהרה נזכה לראות בהרמת קרן התורה וישראל ומלאה הארץ דעת את ה' בביאת גוא"צ בב"א.

הכו"ח לכבוד התורה ולומדי', ולכבוד המחבר שליט"א.

Free translation:

I have been shown a manuscript of the *sefer*, *Emunas Itecha*, by the great and illustrious scholar, famous for his eloquence and virtue, Rav Moshe Wolfson *shlita*, spiritual leader of Congregation *Emunas Yisroel* and *Mashgiach Ruchani* of Mesivta Torah VeDaas in Brooklyn, New York. His remarkable *divrei Torah* in the areas of *drush* and *aggadah* have been widely acclaimed, for they reveal an extraordinary ability to integrate and harmonize the teachings of Chassidus, Mussar, and the deeper aspects of Jewish philosophy. These *divrei Torah* contain lofty and elaborate constructions of thought, and they are as sweet and delightful as a mixture of spices and perfumes; they bring light to the eyes and joy to the heart of those who study them. There is no question that these *divrei Torah* have the power to awaken the heart to Torah, repentance, and good deeds.

It is well known that the author's words and deeds are intended purely for the benefit of his fellow Jews, to bring them closer to the light of Torah and the service of God. Since he has expressed an interest in printing his *divrei Torah* to make them available to a wider audience, I want to encourage him in this endeavor and to express my public acclaim for his writings. His spoken *divrei Torah* have been received with enthusiasm and pleasure by many people, and there will definitely be an appreciative audience for his words in print.

May it be God's Will that just as the author's words were spoken from a pure heart, so should they enter the holy hearts of Israel, to strengthen those who are weak and bring them closer to the service of God. May we soon merit to see the elevation of the Torah and the Jewish people, when the earth will be filled with the knowledge of God, with the arrival of *Moshiach Tsidkeinu*, speedily and in our days, *Amen*.

Rav Yitschok Yaakov Weiss
Rav and *Av Beis Din*
in the Holy City of Jerusalem

ישראל מרדכי בהרה"צ מוהרי"ר יוחנן
זצוקללה"ה טווערסקי
מראחמיסטריווקע - ירושלים עיה"ק ת"ו
ת. ד. 6719
רחוב שפת אמת 6

בעזה"י

כ"ד תמוז תשמ"ז פעיה"ק ירושלים ת"ו

הובא לפני ספר **אמונת עתיך** פרי הגיגו של הרה"ג המפורסם דולה ומשקה תורה לעדרים
וכו' מוה"ר רב **משה וואלפסאן** שליט"א.

הרה"ג הנ"ל רבים שותים בצמא את דבריו ובודאי תועלת למעיינים בדבריו וכו', ואמינא
לפעלא טבא איישר.

יה"ר שיפוצו מעייונתיו חוצה וחפץ ה' בידו יצליח ונזכה במהרה לשמוח בישועת עולמים
בב"א.

Free translation:

B'H
27 Tammuz, 5747

I have been shown the sefer, *Emunas Itecha,* by the renowned scholar
Rav Moshe Wolfson *shlita,* who has worked long and successfully to
make the life-giving waters of the Torah available to the Jewish
people.

For many, the pleasure and benefit of hearing his words has been
like that of a thirsty man discovering water. Since there is much to be
gained by studying the author's words carefully, I give my approval
and encouragement to the project of publishing his *divrei Torah.*

May it be G-d's Will that the author's wellsprings should flow
outwards, that he should succeed in his holy work, and that we
should soon rejoice in the Eternal Redemption, quickly and in our
days, *Amen.*

Yisroel Mordechai,
son of our master and teacher,
Rav Yochanan, זצוקללה"ה

In loving memory of my grandparents

לעילוי נשמת

מיכאל ע״ה   ברוך בן ציון בן חיים צבי הירש ע״ה
Mr. Max Fieldsteel   *Dr. Benjamin Diamond*

בילא ריזל בת יצחק ע״ה   ליבא בת אהרן ע״ה
Mrs. Bella Fieldsteel   *Mrs. Lillian Diamond*

In loving memory of my mother

ברכה סאבל בת רב שלמה אלעזר ז״ל

by

Rabbi Chaim Dovid Brecher

Translator's Foreword

A glimpse of light. A catalyst for spiritual growth. The *divrei Torah* of Rav Moshe Wolfson have provided this for many Jews. Some describe their first encounter with these *divrei Torah* as a turning point in their lives, a step that led them to a deeper commitment to the service of God. For many, it was the discovery of a new level of understanding in Torah, a first taste of the sweetness of Chassidus, a hint at the luminous treasures of Kabbalah. For others it was a revelation no less important: a new awareness of how those exalted levels of wisdom can help us to serve God with enthusiasm and joy.

Until now, these *divrei Torah* have been available to only a small audience. Rav Wolfson generally speaks in Yiddish, and although many of his talks have been translated into Hebrew (*Sefer Emunas Itecha* vol. 1–3, and annual collections starting in 5740), these *sefarim* have not been widely distributed and they are difficult for some readers. Written in a terse and poetic style with many levels of allusions, they contain such a wealth of Torah that readers who are encountering these profound ideas for the first time may need additional explanations. For these readers, and for the many more who do not read Hebrew at all, this translation is an attempt to make a few of these *divrei Torah* accessible.

Rav Wolfson's message and approach are preeminently suitable for a wide audience. His goal and his method are to be *mekareiv* — to bring the listener closer to God, and he speaks with a freshness and a sincerity that is appealing to both the beginner and the accomplished scholar. Although he often refers to the most profound ideas, to the very secrets of the Torah, there is nothing esoteric or intimidating about his approach. He speaks in a way that tells the listener: You may not be able to understand these ideas deeply, but you don't have to be afraid of them. They belong to you — in fact, they describe the deepest levels of your own being. They can bring a new vitality into your soul and a new appreciation for Torah and mitzvos.

The method of these *divrei Torah* is one of explanation and connection: they connect the most elevated ideas with the demands of ordinary life and they show how these ideas can strengthen us. Chapter 3, for example, describes the spiritual connection between every Jew and the *Avos ha-kedoshim*. We discover that the lowest souls are connected with the highest, and that this connection provides an eternal reservoir of faith. The highest ideas are brought down to the level of the reader, and at the same time the reader is lifted up.

Some of the greatest scholars of our time have commented on the extraordinary quality of these *divrei Torah*. For one thing, they are full of *ahavas Yisrael* — a genuine love for the individual Jew with all his imperfections and shortcomings. One senses a compassion and a pity for every Jew, and an attitude of great respect. There is an awareness of the inestimable value of what the simplest Jew can accomplish, the preciousness of the tiniest effort in the service of God. The *ahavas Yisrael* here is also a love of Yiddishkeit, a love for the condition of being Jewish.

Rav Wolfson speaks in a tone that is informal and personal, often with a touch of gentle humor. The goal is to teach, but the approach is never heavy or didactic. These are not a lectures about belief, but personal conversations with a believer. The method is not to argue, but to show. "I am not interested in debating," Rav Wolfson once told me, "but in showering the reader with new ideas." In a deeper sense, what he allows the reader to see is an example of faith, a glimpse into a world of radiance.

These *divrei Torah* have been described as "a mixture of Chassidus and Mussar in a manner of sweetness," and this sweetness is one of their most remarkable qualities. "Taste and see that God is good," David Ha-Melech writes in *Tehillim*, which means there is a way of knowing God that starts with a tangible experience of sweetness. So too, when we listen to Rav Wolfson speak, we can taste the sweetness of Torah. It has been said that Chassidus reveals the goodness of goodness and the truth of truth, and Rav Wolfson accomplishes this by allowing the reader to taste the sweetness of both.

Rav Wolfson's approach is eclectic and tolerant, even as his message is unified. This too makes his message suitable for a very wide audience. Drawing on an extraordinary range of sources, he quotes extensively from all branches of Torah: Midrash and Zohar, Chassidus and Mussar, to name a few. When he cites a source, he is faithful to its true meaning, and at the same time he points out the aspect that is appropriate to his listener. This tolerance for diversity, this ability to create unity by discovering the good in each divergent particular, is also evident among those who have been influenced by Rav Wolfson's teachings. His students include many different varieties of Chassidim and non-Chassidim, adherents of diverse schools of thought and custom, and they all work together in a remarkable atmosphere of mutual respect and *ahavas Yisrael*.

Rav Wolfson's *divrei Torah* are meant to encourage Jews in the service of G-d and to strengthen them in matters of faith. Faith is the very foundation of Judaism. It gives a vitality that can help a person perform all the mitzvos, as it is written

(*Chavakuk* 2:4): "The righteous will live by his faith." In our time, the task of strengthening faith is particularly urgent. As the *talmidim* of the Baal Shem Tov have told us, it is the area in which we confront the greatest challenges, and it is where our success is of the utmost importance. Hence there is a vital need to bring Rav Wolfson's message of encouragement to as many Jews as possible, and that is the goal of this translation.

A note about how was this translation was prepared: It was clear from the beginning that a line-by-line translation of the *Sefer Emunas Itecha* would not be sufficient. To present such profound ideas to a wide audience, it would be necessary to provide explanations and illustrations. Inferences and allusions that were only hinted at in the Hebrew would have to be stated explicitly, and in some places it would be necessary to add introductions and summaries. In short, it was clear that the translator would have to function like a good teacher, first internalizing the material and then presenting it in his own words. Rav Wolfson's advice was: "Write as creatively as possible."

At the same time, Rav Wolfson supervised the work closely. Rough drafts, with hundreds of questions, were faxed over the Atlantic, and Rav Wolfson generously took the time to respond with corrections, clarifications, and additions. When the final draft of the book was ready, it was shown to him again for approval.

This *sefer* is based primarily, but not exclusively, on *divrei Torah* that are found in *Sefer Emunas Itecha,* in the chapters on *Sefer Bereishis* and Chanukah. Most of the material was chosen by the translator, with the subsequent approval of Rav Wolfson. One *dvar Torah* was selected by Rav Wolfson himself — the *ma'amar, Moriah and Machpeilah,* which appears in *Sefer Emunas Itecha* on *parashas Chayei Sarah.* It is translated here in its entirety, with only minor omissions and rearrangements, and it forms the longest chapter of this *sefer*, Chapter 3. Chapters 2, 4, and 5 are also based primarily on selections from *Sefer Emunas Itecha*.

In addition, the translator listened to many tape recordings of talks (some in English and some in Yiddish), in which Rav Wolfson presented these *divrei Torah*. Chapter 1 is based primarily on such a recording, and some material from these tapes was also used in other chapters.

It should be obvious that this *sefer* presents only a tiny sample of Rav Wolfson's *divrei Torah*. In terms of style and tone, the selections here are fairly typical. In terms of content, however, this is no more than a *minchas oni*, a pauper's offering. Rav Wolfson's *divrei Torah* contain a tremendous wealth of ideas and a range of topics that are not even hinted at in this collection. It hoped that this *sefer* will provide a taste of the sweetness and the richness that are found in his *divrei Torah*, and that readers will then go on to discover this for themselves.

It should also be noted that each of the *divrei Torah* in this collection was originally said separately and independently. Each speaks about a particular *sedrah* or *Yom Tov*, and each follows its own internal logic. In choosing these *divrei Torah*, the primary criterion was the individual appeal of each one, and there was little attempt to mold the pieces into a larger pattern.

One minor exception to this rule is found in Chapter 5, where a brief introduction and a conclusion were added by the translator. This was suggested by an editor in order to link the final chapter more closely with the rest of the *sefer*, and it goes without saying that the additions were approved by Rav Wolfson. As a general rule, however, each *dvar Torah* was allowed to stand on its own.

There are, of course, a number of common themes that appear and reappear throughout the book. Most of these are related to faith, and so this *sefer* can be described as a collection of *divrei Torah* on the topic of faith.

In addition, as the work progressed, another unifying idea became apparent. Many of the questions discussed in these *divrei Torah* seem to be related to a tension that is implicit in the title of Rav Wolfson's Hebrew *sefer*: *Emunas Itecha*. *Emunah* means faith, and faith is by definition unchanging. The very word *emunah* means steady and unwavering, as in the Torah's description of Moshe Rabbeinu's leadership in the war against *Amalek*: *va-yehi yadav emunah*, "his hands were steady" (*Shemos* 17:12). In contrast, the word *itecha* means "your times" or "your seasons," and so it conveys the idea of time and change.

Faith exists within the world of time and change, and nevertheless, it transcends time. This is a fact, albeit a mysterious one. *Emunah* exists within *itecha*, and yet it is beyond it. The question of how this occurs is touched upon many times in these *divrei Torah*. On an individual level, it is also the question of how faith can grow and develop during a person's lifetime. To be sure, as we said earlier, these are not lectures on Jewish philosophy, and Rav Wolfson does not discuss such questions in the abstract. Nevertheless, a thoughtful reader may sense that this mystery, the relation between faith and time, is present beneath the surface of many of these *divrei Torah*.

In some individuals the light of faith shines more brightly, and when such a person shares his faith with others, the light moves outwards and downwards, and faith is revealed in a new location. In a similar way, every act of expression and every act of writing involves a movement outwards and downwards, as private thought is translated into the public domain of language.

One of the challenges of writing is to ensure that the public expression remains faithful to the private truth that inspired it, and when ideas are translated into a different language, the issue of fidelity is particularly important. In bringing an author's ideas into a foreign language, a translator may have to work within the terms and assumptions of a culture whose way of looking at the world is profoundly different from that of the author. And yet, even on that foreign terrain, a faithful translation can reveal the essence of the author's ideas.

Rav Wolfson's *divrei Torah* are an expression of faith, and they are meant to bring the light of faith outwards and downwards, to a new location. In this respect, the process of translating these *divrei Torah* is a natural extension and implementation of their original intention. Thus, a faithful translation of Rav Wolfson's words should also provide an outward movement of faith itself. It is my hope and prayer that this *sefer* will contribute towards that goal.

* * *

The realm of holiness is characterized by a clear recognition of the Divine source of existence. Celestial beings are vividly aware that their life and energies are channeled to them from above, and so their awareness of themselves is diminished. Even when they reflect upon their own abilities, they see in them only God's beneficence. Human beings can also approach this level. When Yaakov Avinu considered all the goodness he had received from Hashem, he exclaimed, *"Katonti mi-kol ha-chasadim..."* — "I have been made small because of all the kindness...You have done for Your servant." As a result of God's kindness, Yaakov became more humble.

Every time we thank Hashem, we move towards a similar transformation of consciousness. We also do this when we thank people who have helped us in our lives and we recognize that our own accomplishments were made possible by their efforts.

Before all else, I thank the Almighty for His abundant kindness to me, to my family, and to His people, Israel. My ability to acknowledge His goodness will always be inadequate in comparison to the magnitude of His blessings, and I consider even the fact that He allows me to praise Him to be one of the greatest expressions of His love.

When we try to express our gratitude to other human beings, we also find our powers of recognition to be inadequate, yet that does not exempt us from our responsibility. A *sefer* like this reaches the public only as a result of the coordinated efforts of many people, both those involved directly and indirectly, and I would like to take this opportunity to thank all of them.

In particular, I would like to thank the *Mashgiach*, Rav Wolfson *shlita*, for his permission to translate these *divrei Torah* into English. It has been a privilege and a responsibility. In addition to his contribution as the author of these *divrei Torah*, Rav Wolfson also supervised the preparation of the translation, which was of great help to me and to the readers. Throughout the project, his encouragement, support, and generosity of spirit were vitally important and greatly appreciated. May Hashem give him many more years of good health and strength to continue guiding the Jewish people in the service of God.

I would also like to express my thanks to the following individuals, *sheyichyu*:

▸ Mr. Yaakov Feldheim for the initial suggestion to translate Rav Wolfson's *divrei Torah* into English, and for his encouragement and assistance along the way.

▸ The *talmidim* of Rav Wolfson, who helped defray the costs of producing this *sefer. Rabbis Chaim Dovid Brecher, Yehudah Gutwein, Hertz Hassenfeld, Aaron Herzog, and Ruvein Rosenberg* made major donations, and other *talmidim* also provided assistance. May Hashem bless them and protect them together with their entire families, and may they find success and satisfaction in all areas of life.

▶ Dr. Uri Cheskin, who read the first draft carefully and suggested many significant improvements.

▶ Rabbi Moshe Wisnefsky, who read a later version of the manuscript and offered many valuable editorial suggestions. He also provided many of the precise references that appear in the footnotes, as well as much valuable advice and support.

▶ Mrs. Suri Brand for a meticulous and professional job of copyediting. Her perceptive comments and closely reasoned suggestions were very helpful in identifying points that needed further clarification.

▶ Mrs. Joyce Bennett, Mrs. Bracha Steinberg, Mrs. Hannah Hartman, and the entire staff at Feldheim publishers in Jerusalem, for their professionalism and patience.

▶ Rabbi Eliezer Shore, who edited a section of the manuscript and provided a number of valuable suggestions.

▶ Rabbi Yirmiyah Zucker for his kindness and encouragement.

▶ Mr. Ben Gasner, who designed the cover.

I would also like to thank my parents, Mr. and Mrs. Ira Fieldsteel *sheyichyu*, and my parents-in-law, Mr. and Mrs. Shmuel Yashar *sheyichyu*, for their kindness and generosity, and for the assistance they provided while I was working on this *sefer*. May Hashem bless them with many more years of good health and with much happiness from their families.

I am especially thankful to my wife Esther *shetichyeh*, for her cooperation and encouragement. Her contribution to this *sefer* is more than just the hard work and dedication at home that helped make it possible for me to complete this translation, it is also the example of *emunah* she provides for our family. May we and our children *sheyichyu* have the merit to give *nachas ruach* to Hashem and to the Jewish people.

In thinking about my work on this *sefer*, I am reminded of my grandfather, Dr. Benjamin Diamond, ברוך בן ציון בן חיים צבי הירש ע"ה, who had a strong influence on my Jewish education. It seems like not so long ago that we were sitting together reading stories in simple Hebrew about Avraham Avinu, as my grandfather tried to teach the rudiments of Hebrew grammar to a young, American boy from the suburbs. Although his success in teaching me Hebrew grammar was limited, I think he may have succeeded in transmitting something far deeper — some faint, intangible essence from the *cheder* in the Ukraine where he studied as a young boy. I feel that he also has a share in the making of this *sefer*.

In his letter of approval to *Sefer Emunas Itecha*, the Rachmistrivka Rebbe, Rav Yisroel Mordechai Twersky *shlita* gave Rav Wolfson the traditional blessing (based on *Mishlei* 5:16): "May his wellsprings spread outwards."

A wellspring is a source of water within the earth, a hidden point from which life-giving waters emerge. Thus the simple meaning of this blessing is that the living, life-giving waters of Rav Wolfson's *divrei Torah* should become more widely available — which is the reason for this translation. Faith is an essential theme in all of Rav Wolfson's *divrei Torah*, and one of his teachings is that the faith of a Jew is derived from wellsprings deep within his soul. Since the goal of this *sefer* is to reveal those wellsprings, and to make the faith that flows from them more widely available, it has been titled *Wellsprings of Faith*.

I would like to close with a prayer that Rav Wolfson himself wrote in his preface to *Sefer Emunas Itecha* (vol. 1), for I feel that it expresses my own feelings about the work at hand:

I entreat my Creator and request from Him that this *sefer*

should benefit those who learn from it, strengthening them in faith, and in the fear of Heaven, and in the development of good character traits. May it be acceptable and pleasing to the readers, and may I too be strengthened and improved by it. May it be God's Will to give help, deliverance, and protection to all those who assisted in the making of this *sefer*, to their families, and to the entire House of Israel. May we merit to serve the Creator, Blessed be He, with truth and sincerity, amidst joy and satisfaction, abundance and contentment, love and friendship, until the arrival of *Mashiach Tzidkeinu*, quickly, in our days, and very soon.

Yehoshua Fieldsteel
Yerushalayim
Zos Chanukah, 5762

Foreword

by Rabbi Shimon Finkelman

Our Sages taught: מורא רבך כמורא שמים — "Reverence for your teacher should be like the reverence for Heaven" (*Avos* 4:15). It is therefore with a profound sense of awe and inadequacy that I write this Foreword to the English-language rendition of the discourses of my *rebbi*, HaRav Moshe Wolfson, *shlita*. Far be it from me to attempt a portrait of this revered *tzaddik* and *manhig* (spiritual leader); what follows is one *talmid*'s attempt to describe his *rebbi*'s impact on the lives of scores of *talmidim* and countless others who strive to grow in their service of Hashem.

HaRav Wolfson has served for decades as *Mashgiach Ruchani* of Mesivta Torah Vodaath, a position for which he was handpicked by the *Rosh Yeshivah*, HaGaon HaRav Yaakov Kamenetsky, *zt"l*. (R' Yaakov is reported to have said that his appointment of HaRav Wolfson to this position was one of his most important achievements as *Rosh Yeshivah*.) To this day, all of us refer to HaRav Wolfson with reverence and love as "the *Mashgiach*." *Talmidim* of Torah Vodaath have always found in him a personage who clearly lives a higher existence, yet who relates so well to the needs and *nisyonos* (spiritual tests) of the typical American yeshivah student. Many who, as young *bachurim*, turned to the *Mashgiach* twenty-five years ago for his keen insight, sage counsel, and fatherly concern, still do so today, as mature adults and men of accomplishment.

The discourses in this volume are drawn from the *Mashgiach's* Hebrew work, *Emunas Itecha*, a collection of *shmuessen* delivered at *Shalosh Seudos* in the *Beis Medrash Emunas Yisroel*, where he serves as *Rav*. The *Mashgiach's* discourses are unique. It is not only his inimitable way of bringing together the four branches of Torah interpretation (פשט, רמז, דרוש, סוד) to form a tapestry that is breathtaking in scope and depth. The *shmuessen* weave the concepts of Chassidic thought with esoteric concepts of *Kabbalah*, the profundities of *Maharal*, and other classic works.

But this, too, does not define their uniqueness. As the hundreds who attend these talks each week will attest, the sum of each *shmuess* is greater than its parts. The listener is treated not only to original interpretations; he gains a new appreciation of the infinite treasures that lie beneath the surface of each word of Torah. His *emunah* is strengthened, his attachment to Torah fortified. He comes away with the inspiration to grow and with a feeling of:

אשרינו מה טוב חלקנו, ומה נעים גורלנו, "We are fortunate — how good is our portion, how pleasant is our lot!"

There is no greater testimony to this inspiration than the very *beis medrash* in which the *shmuessen* are delivered. From a handful of *talmidim* of the *Mashgiach* twenty-five years ago, *Emunas Yisroel* has grown to become a *kehillah* of some two hundred families (כן ירבו). But more important, *Emunas Yisroel* has become a spiritual landmark in the heart of Boro Park, a neighborhood filled with scores of shuls and yeshivos. It has become known far and wide as a place where *tefillah* is a true service of the heart and where respect for *tefillah* and the sanctity of the *beis medrash* results in perfect decorum — even among children and for the duration of a three-hour Shabbos morning *tefillah.*

Emunas Yisroel is also a center of Torah learning, with the sounds of study reverberating from early morning until past midnight. And it is a center of *chesed,* where the needy find succor and support, where people struck by tragedy, ר״ל, find friendship and warmth. It is a place where a weary, overburdened visitor from Jerusalem, or a *baal teshuvah* from Russia or Rhode Island, feels welcome.

It is a place of spiritual ecstasy on the nights of Purim and Simchas Torah, and at *ne'ilas hachag,* the concluding *seudah* of *Yom Tov,* when the "regulars" are joined by scores of "outsiders" who yearn to experience the *simchah shel mitzvah* which is the essence of a *Yom Tov. Emunas Yisroel* is a "melting pot" of sorts, a panorama of chassidim joined by products of Lithuanian yeshivos, in mutual respect and unity.

All this is primarily due to the inspiration of the *Mashgiach,* both through his personality and his *shmuessen.* Since his weekly talks are delivered in Yiddish,* it is a source of great joy that a collection of his *shmuessen* have now been made available to the English reader in this beautiful volume, written by a *talmid* of the *Mashgiach,* Rabbi Yehoshua Fieldsteel. Rabbi Fieldsteel's work is faithful to the original, and he has succeeded in presenting abstract concepts in a clear, readable style. I might add that the *Mashgiach's* style is poetic and musical, and Rabbi Fieldsteel succeeds in conveying the beauty of the presentation, as well as the profundity of the content.

We are greatful to Rabbi Yaakov Feldheim, who after being present at a *shmuess* delivered by the *Mashgiach* in Jerusalem, initiated this project and saw it through to completion.

I take this opportunity to express my *hakaras hatov* to the

---

* Tapes of about forty English discourses can be ordered by calling 718-436-0873 or 718-633-8752.

Mashgiach for all that he has done for me and for the impact that he has had on my family. I know that I speak for all the *Mashgiach's* *talmidim* as I offer a *tefillah* that Hashem grant him many more healthy and productive years אמן עד ביאת גואל צדק במהרה בימנו.

Contents

1.

THE ORIGINS OF FAITH
AVRAHAM, THE FIRST BELIEVER

When we reach the week in which *Parashas Lech Lecha* is read, a new star is visible in the heavens, for this is the moment when we welcome the arrival of Avraham Avinu.

The arrival of Avraham is a turning point in the history of the world — a moment that is both a beginning and a conclusion. It is a beginning, because Avraham is an entirely new type of person and the nation he fathers is a new type of nation. But it is also a conclusion, because Avraham's arrival represents the culmination of a long process of creation and development. It is only at this point in history, our Sages tell us, that God's work of Creation comes to its intended conclusion. Though the process of Creation began at the dawn of time, its goal was realized only two thousand years later, with the arrival of Avraham Avinu and the birth of the Jewish people.

Our Sages find an echo of this idea in the verse that follows the Torah's account of the creation of the world. In the opening chapters of the Torah, the six days of Creation are described in detail, and the seventh day, Shabbos, is announced and sanctified. Then the Torah begins a new paragraph אלה תולדות השמים והארץ בהבראם — "This is the history of

1

the heavens and the earth when they were created."[1]

At this point, the Torah seems to be looking back at the completed work of Creation and making a statement that is no more than a summary. However, there is an important insight here, a clue to the very meaning of Creation. If we look carefully at the word בהבראם, *Chazal* tell us,[2] we find that it is the Hebrew name אברהם — Avraham, with the letters rearranged.

In its literal sense, בהבראם means "in their being created," and thus it refers to and recapitulates the entire work of Creation. But the word also contains, as it were, its own commentary. Why was the world created? For what purpose? It was created so that there would be an Avraham. The true reason for Creation is hidden from our eyes when we look at the world, just as the name Avraham is hidden in the word בהבראם. "Consider the heavens and earth, which were just created," the Torah tells us, "and know that they were created בהבראם — because of Avraham."

What was so special about Avraham that he was considered the purpose of Creation, the reason why Hashem created the world?

Avraham Avinu was an entirely new type of person. In fact, his nature was so radically different and original that it is an understatement to describe him simply as a new *type* of person. In addition, when we recognize that Avraham was able to transmit this new nature to his descendants and to make it a permanent part of the character of the Jewish people, we might go so far as to say that he represents the beginning of a new human "species" — the Jewish species.[3]

---

1. *Bereshis* 2:4.
2. *Bereshis Rabbah* 12.
3. See pp. 22–26, "A People Defined by Faith," where this idea is developed and used to answer to a number of questions about Avraham.

But what was so original about Avraham? What new element appeared for the first time in him? The answer, in one word, is *emunah*, faith. Indeed, the very first time the word *emunah* appears in the Torah is in connection with Avraham: והאמן בה' ויחשבה לו צדקה — "*He believed* in Hashem, and He [Hashem] regarded it as righteousness."[4] Thus Avraham Avinu was the first person to serve Hashem through *emunah*. But to understand this, we must know more about *emunah*.

THE BOOTSTRAP COMMAND

One of the commandments of the Torah is the mitzvah of *emunah*, the mitzvah to believe in Hashem. There is, however, an essential difference between this mitzvah and every other mitzvah of the Torah: The Torah never gives us a direct command to believe in Hashem; it does not say, "You shall believe."

All the other mitzvos, in contrast, are written as imperatives, generally phrased as either a "do" or a "don't." For example, we recite Kiddush on Shabbos because the Torah commands us, "Remember the Shabbos day in order to sanctify it."[5] We are warned against eating nonkosher food with the words, "Do not eat any abominable thing."[6]

According to the Rambam, the mitzvah of *emunah* is found in the Torah in the first verse of the Ten Commandments: "I am Hashem, your God...."[7] Clearly this is not the usual language of a command. Grammatically it is a simple declarative sentence, with no word that directly tells us to perform an action or even to think a particular thought. Nevertheless, based

---

4. *Bereshis* 15:6.
5. *Shemos* 20:7.
6. *Devarim* 14:3.
7. *Shemos* 20:2.

on this verse the Rambam counts the mitzvah of *emunah* as one of the 613 mitzvos. In fact, he lists it as the first of all the mitzvos.[8]

There is a dissenting opinion, however — that of the Ramban.[9] He maintains that we cannot count the mitzvah of *emunah* as one of the 613 mitzvos, since *emunah* is a pre-condition for all the mitzvos. First one must accept God's existence, and only then can one accept the obligation to carry out His will. First one must know that there is a *Metzaveh*, a Commander, and only then can there be a mitzvah, a commandment. Thus for the Ramban *emunah* is much more than a mitzvah; it is the foundation upon which the entire structure of Torah and mitzvos is based.

Both views consider *emunah* to be an essential part of our service of God. But the Rambam's opinion presents us with a problem: If *emunah* is to be counted with the other mitzvos, as he states, why doesn't the Torah state it in a similar way, in the language of a command? To answer this question as well, we will have to look more deeply at the nature of *emunah*.

TWO TYPES OF KNOWLEDGE

Acquired Knowledge

Throughout our lives, we are constantly acquiring new knowledge. When we read a book, for example, we gain information from the printed page. It is knowledge we did not have before, and now we make it a part of ourselves. This knowledge, however, is not something our children will be born with. Since it comes from a source outside ourselves, it will not be transmitted through heredity. Our children will have this knowledge only if they make an effort to learn it themselves. In other

---

8. *Sefer Ha-Mitzvos, Mitzvos Aseh* 1.
9. Commentary to *Sefer Ha-Mitzvos*, ad loc.

words, acquired knowledge is not hereditary.

Hereditary Knowledge

There are, however, certain types of knowledge and intelligence that are hereditary, and they can be transmitted to the next generation by biological processes alone. This knowledge seems to be packaged in the chromosomes, recorded in a marvelously small and precise script and enciphered in the mysterious language of the genes. This is one of the great wonders of the *Ribbono shel Olam* — among the millions of other wonders around us, which we can appreciate by using the intelligence the Creator has bestowed on us.

There are many examples of hereditary knowledge. A beaver, for instance, knows how to build a dam in the middle of a stream, and it does a remarkably good job of it. We could not build a dam like that without a course in civil engineering. Yet the beaver does it without any training at all. Even a beaver raised in captivity, who never saw even a picture of a dam, will be able to build one as soon as it is freed and returned to its natural environment.

How does the beaver know how to build a dam? It was equipped with the necessary knowledge from birth — through heredity.

Consider the ability of a spider to spin a web. Spiders hatch from eggs, and so a baby spider may never even see its mother. And yet, that spider will be able to build a web as easily as its mother did, and with exactly the same pattern. Building a web is just part of being a spider. It's in the blood — or, as we say today, it's in the chromosomes.

Many species of birds migrate every fall to a warmer climate. They have the extraordinary ability to travel for thousands of miles and then to return in the spring, six months later, to the very same tree in the same backyard. We, who call ourselves *Homo sapiens* because of our ability to think, would find it impossible to duplicate this feat without an array of sophisticated equipment. How do they accomplish this wonder? Do they remember every river and road, every meadow and valley, over a journey of thousands of miles? Do they navigate by the stars, or by the rising and setting of the sun?

A bird, although it cannot think abstractly, is endowed with a special memory and a talent for navigation. Of course, the bird does not understand these abilities. Even a human being, who knows how to think abstractly, cannot really explain them. It is an ability the bird has just by virtue of being a bird. It is hereditary knowledge.

Human beings are also born with certain types of hereditary intelligence. A newborn baby, for example, knows how to nurse. The baby knows that it must form a vacuum with its mouth in order to suck, and without this it would not be able to eat. Without ever having studied physics, a baby knows the law of the vacuum, although, of course, it cannot express this knowledge in the language of science.

Thus we come to the conclusion that there are two types of knowledge: acquired knowledge is obtained by an individual through his own efforts, while hereditary knowledge is unearned, a "gift" from earlier generations. Hereditary knowledge belongs to a person before he even knows how to ask for it. And it can serve him faithfully without the assistance, or even the awareness, of his conscious mind. Hereditary knowledge, in short, belongs to a person not because of what he *does*, but because of what he *is*.

Similarly, there are two types of knowledge or belief in God, one acquired and the other hereditary.

TWO TYPES OF BELIEF IN GOD

Rational Belief

It is possible to acquire a belief in the *Ribbono shel Olam* through reason and understanding. By using one's intellect to examine the world, one can come to recognize the One God, Who created everything.

This pathway to belief is available to all human beings, not only Jews, and for this reason, every individual is expected to believe in the *Ribbono shel Olam*. Indeed, our Sages tell us that the gentile nations will ultimately be taken to task for their failure to believe in one God. This is because, as Rav Elchonon Wasserman explains, everything in the universe points to the existence of one God. Our world is so wonderful, and so clearly the product of design, that one can recognize the Creator even by means of intellect alone.[10]

It is not necessary to study the distant galaxies to recognize the handiwork of the Creator, nor does one have to track the exotic behavior of subatomic particles in the arcane world of the infinitesimally small. Even on a familiar scale the universe testifies to its Creator. Even that small corner of creation where we feel so comfortably at home — the human body — offers such a dazzling display of marvels and wonders that a person who reflects on them honestly must be led to a recognition of the Creator. As Iyov declared, "From my own body I can see God."[11]

I once had the opportunity to look through a medical student's textbook of anatomy and physiology. It was astonishing and inspiring, a veritable atlas of wonders. The book consisted of hundreds of pages with twenty or thirty marvels on every page. There were intricate explanations of the most subtle de-

---

10. *Kuntras Ikvesa d'Meshicha.*
11. *Iyov* 19:26.

tails in the construction of the human body.

Consider, for example, the curvature of the human spine. It bulges backward at the shoulders, forward at the abdomen, and then back out again. It had never occurred to me to ask why, but there is a very good reason for it. If the spine were perfectly straight, then when a person jumped and landed on his feet the full force of his fall would suddenly push the upper vertebrae down on the lower ones. There would be nothing to cushion the shock. Since the spine is S-shaped, however, it bends like a resilient and elastic bow, and the impact is safely absorbed.

Every part of the body is full of wonders. Is there a camera on the market that can begin to compete with the eye? What camera has its own built-in repair system? The eye does, as well as other sophisticated systems for maintenance and protection. The tear glands constantly wash the eye clean, and the eyelids and eyelashes protect it from foreign particles. If an object comes flying through the air toward a person's face, his eyelids will close automatically and his arm will jump up to protect his eyes, because the eyes need more protection than the arm. And this happens before a person has time to think — the reflexes of his nervous system do the thinking for him.

In fact, it is known today that the eye is much more than a camera. It performs many functions that modern technology can imitate only with computers. The retina is not merely a passive recording device like a piece of film; there are circuits and systems of nerves within the retina that actively interpret the patterns of light it is presented with. Some circuits respond, for example, to moving images; others recognize borders and shapes.

When we turn our attention to the higher-level processes of visual perception that take place within the brain — one of the simpler examples might be binocular vision — we have to admit that we have entered the realm of genuine miracles and profound mysteries.

But even when we consider biological processes that are somewhat more comprehensible, we find that the very complexity of the body and the interdependence of its parts adds up to a miracle that is nearly incomprehensible. Let us again consider the eye. The eye cannot function unless it is supplied with blood. So we are endowed with a circulatory system — a heart, blood vessels, and millions of microscopic capillaries that bring the blood to the eyes as well as to all the other organs of the body. The blood carries oxygen and food to the entire body. But where does the oxygen come from? To answer this question we would have to explore the respiratory system, another organized kingdom of miracles. And how does the food enter the bloodstream? That is the job of the digestive system, an equally fantastic array of recurring wonders. The body is a network of millions of interactions and interdependencies. Every organ of the body is itself a wonder, but the way they all work together in harmony is a far greater wonder — and every day new wonders are being discovered.

As a result, medical researchers take it for granted that every part of the body has a function. The body itself has taught them to think this way. Many features of anatomy and physiology which once seemed arbitrary or strange are now known to be perfectly designed for functions that scientists in earlier generations never even dreamed of.

This is why, commenting on the verse *"Ein tzur k'Elokenu,"*[12] which means literally, "There is no Rock like our God," the Gemara[13] suggests an additional level of meaning. We are invited to read this as: *"Ein tzayar k'Elokenu* — There is

---

12. *Shmuel* I 2:2.
13. *Berachos* 10a.

no *artist* like our God." And the best evidence of God's artistic genius is the human body, with its multitude of internal and external organs all working together in harmony. When we contemplate this inscrutably marvelous piece of craftsmanship, we are led to the recognition that it is the product of a Divine wisdom, and this teaches us to see the entire world as an expression of God's wisdom, planning, and purpose.

So we do not have to go beyond ourselves to know that there is a God Who created the world. We do not have to investigate the stars or the planets or the wonders of botany and zoology. "From my own body I can see God." And therefore, even a non-Jew is expected to believe in the *Ribbono shel Olam*.

Hereditary Belief

There is, however, an entirely different type of belief in God — the belief with which a Jew is born. Every Jew knows there is a God in the same instinctive way he knows how to breathe. He doesn't have to be taught it, and he doesn't have to figure it out through logic. It is a knowledge that comes from the deepest level of his being. He may not be able to justify this knowledge intellectually or even to articulate it clearly, but it is there, within him. It is hereditary knowledge.[14]

Just as migratory birds have a homing instinct, every Jew has an innate sense of direction, a built-in compass that directs him toward his Source — toward his Father in Heaven. Just as a newborn infant knows how to draw life-giving milk from its mother, every Jew is born with an instinct that prompts him to draw life from the Source of all life — from God.

The idea that human beings have access to certain kinds of

---

14. A well-known exposition of this idea is found in the *Kuzari*, but the idea itself is from *Chazal*. It is hinted at, for example, in our Sages' description of the Jewish people as *ma'aminim u-venei ma'aminim*, "believers and the sons of believers."

unconscious, instinctive knowledge is not just a theoretical concept. In Torah, even the most abstract and esoteric truths often have practical consequences, and this truth is no exception. It makes its way into legal discussions on topics of the utmost gravity. Let us consider a case in which this idea plays a decisive role.

The Torah says that if a person finds a burglar breaking into his house, he is entitled to protect his property, even if he has to kill the intruder in order to do so.[15] The justification for this is as follows:

The burglar is certainly aware that the occupant of the house may try to defend his property, and hence we can assume that the burglar is prepared to use violence. Since this violence could lead to the death of the homeowner, the Torah regards the burglar, from the outset, as a mortal threat. Hence, in accordance with the principle of self-defense, the homeowner is justified in killing the burglar when there is no other way to stop him.

If, however, we had a case in which one of these assumptions no longer held true, the conclusion would also be invalid. If, for example, we could be certain that the burglar would not kill the homeowner, the whole chain of reasoning would come to a halt. It would then be forbidden to use lethal force against the burglar. Indeed, *Chazal* tell us,[16] this is precisely the situation when the burglar is the father of the homeowner. A father — even a father willing to steal from his own child — would never kill his child. Therefore, if a person were to discover his own father breaking into his house, he would not be permitted to kill him, because his father does not pose a threat to his life.

Keeping this case in mind, let us now consider one addi-

---

15. *Shemos* 22:1; *Sanhedrin* 72a.
16. *Shemos* 22:2; *Sanhedrin* 72b.

tional complication. What if the burglar does not realize that the homeowner is his son? Imagine, for example, that someone has just moved into a new house, and his own father — who is completely unaware of the move — chooses that house for his next burglary. What is the halachah in such a case, when the homeowner knows that the burglar is his father, but the burglar does not know that the homeowner is his son? Would the homeowner then be permitted to kill his father in self-defense?

"Absolutely not!" answers the Chasam Sofer,[17] one of the great halachic authorities, and he offers an astonishing explanation for his ruling. Instinct will always prevent a father from killing his son — even in a case like this one, where the father is unaware that the other person is his child.

This is truly remarkable! Consider the implications: The burglar believes the homeowner to be a complete stranger, and on the level of conscious knowledge, he is making a mistake. But on the level of instinct, the Chasam Sofer tells us, on the level of hereditary knowledge, he knows the truth. His instinct in this case is more sensitive, more accurate, and more dependable than his intellect.

And that is not all. Not only does the burglar know the truth by instinct, but that truth will actually determine his actions. He will not be able to kill the homeowner! He himself will not understand why, and it will not make logical sense to him, but something deep within him will prevent him from killing his son. His instinct will overpower his intellect.

Why does this instinctive knowledge only make itself felt at such a critical and desperate moment? The answer is that the child's life is at risk, and hence the entire connection between parent and child is in jeopardy. This connection lives within

---

17. *Chiddushei Chasam Sofer* on *Pesachim* 2a, s.v. *"l'or yakum rotzeiach."*

the parent; it is part of his identity as a parent, and at such a moment it is threatened.

Normally this instinctive knowledge is hidden and quiescent. It is a kind of self-knowledge, the self-awareness of the parent-child relationship, the consciousness of a shared, inner identity. And, as a kind of self-awareness, a knowledge derived from being, it is generally united with being. It does not usually express itself outwardly, for outward expression is a movement away from its natural inward unity. It is like the quiet, dormant fire of a glowing coal, a fire united with its source.

But at a moment of crisis, at a moment when the inner identity which sustains the knowledge is subject to a mortal threat, that instinctive self-knowledge will awaken and move outward with great force. An awareness that had never ventured even into the world of thought suddenly seizes the reins of power and dictates action. The coal bursts into flame, and the flame becomes a raging fire with the power to consume any threat to that true, inner identity.[18]

Thus, as the Chasam Sofer clearly tells us, there is a kind of hereditary knowledge that is not only independent of the conscious mind, but also more accurate, and it has the power, at times, to override the conscious mind and direct a person's actions.

There is another kind of instinctive recognition: the recognition of an animal for its owner, as the prophet Yeshayahu declares, "An ox recognizes its owner, and a donkey knows its master's feeding trough."[19] The very fact of belonging gives an animal the ability to recognize its master and his property. The

---

18. See *Tanya, Likutei Amarim*, ch. 30, for a similar description of the soul's innate knowledge of God.
19. *Yeshayahu* 1:3.

verse continues with the prophet exclaming in amazement, "Doesn't the Jewish people know?"

"You are much wiser than the animals," the prophet is saying to *klal Yisrael*, "and God is much more to you than an Owner; you are His children.[20] So don't you know who your Father in Heaven is?"

Just as there is an instinctive recognition between an animal and its owner, the prophet tells us, so too every Jew has an instinctive recognition of God. A Jew needs only to awaken this instinctive knowledge, and it will reconnect him with his Father in Heaven.

SO HOW CAN A JEW DISBELIEVE?

We have come to understand that the word *emunah* does not refer to a knowledge based on the evaluation of evidence and experience. That is what we have called "rational belief." Rather, *emunah* means the hereditary knowledge of God that a Jew is born with, an instinctive knowledge like the natural recognition between a parent and a child. Since *emunah* is hereditary, we can trace its inheritance back in time, from each generation to the one before. Where does this search lead us? It leads us to the first link, to the beginning — to Avraham. As our Sages tell us, Avraham was the *rosh la-ma'aminim*, the first believer.[21]

There is a general principle that the *rosh*, or the beginning of a process, actually generates what comes later. Here too, Avraham was not merely the first believer; he was the *father* of all believers. Later generations were believers because they inherited their belief from him. Avraham was the father of all believers and the father of belief itself. Due to Avraham, every

---

20. בנים אתם לד׳ אלקיכם — see *Devarim* 14:1.
21. See *Shir Ha-Shirim Rabbah* 4:3.

Jewish soul is endowed with *emunah* as a natural inheritance.

Unfortunately, however, even a natural inheritance can be damaged. Just as the physical body can be damaged by sickness or abuse, so can the soul, the spiritual organism, become damaged.

The Rambam tells us that if we want to understand spiritual illness, we can look at physical illness as a model. Let us consider, for example, the appetite for food. When a healthy person goes for more than a few hours without eating, he feels hungry. But what would happen to a person who started eating a bowl of sawdust and milk for breakfast every morning? Without a doubt, he would become ill. His stomach would stop functioning, and his normal appetite would disappear. Thus when the body is sick, even its instinctive responses can be disrupted.

What would that person have to do in order to regain his health? First of all, he would have to stop eating the sawdust which is making him sick. And then, depending on how much damage had already occurred, he might need medical treatment. With proper care, his body would recover, and his appetite would return.

Similar processes can also occur within the spiritual organism, the *neshamah*. The healthy Jewish soul has an instinctive belief in God. But if someone damages his *neshamah* through spiritual abuse, he could become spiritually ill, and the natural powers of his soul, including the power of *emunah*, would be weakened. What is the definition of "spiritual abuse"? The answer can be stated in one word: sin.

Spiritual Sclerosis

Every *aveirah*, every sin, can damage the soul and weaken the faculty of *emunah*. "Sin stupefies the heart," Chazal tell us.[22] Sin dulls the spiritual heart and numbs the natural recognition by which a Jew knows his Father in Heaven.

If fat and cholesterol accumulate in the arteries that supply blood to a person's heart, he would be told to reduce the cholesterol in his diet and to take medicines that will help clear the arteries. Sometimes, depending on the degree of damage, he might even need a bypass operation to restore the normal flow of blood to the heart.

Similarly, the spiritual heart can become clogged — not by cholesterol, but by *aveiros*. Sin interferes with the natural flow of holiness within the heart and renders the heart hard and unresponsive. The Jewish heart is designed by the Creator to be an instrument of exquisite sensitivity, one capable of responding to the most delicate tremors of holiness. It is meant to resonate with the love and fear of God in a thousand subtle variations of tone and timbre. It has the ability to sing before the Creator with a range and register that no symphony orchestra can match. But sin clogs and occludes. It closes what ought to be open, and it opens what ought to be closed. Suddenly a voice that was singing the harmonies of Heaven is transposed downward into a scale of untempered dissonance, a key of half-steps and halting discord.

But just as a particular organ of the body can be damaged by some diseases and remain unaffected by others, the soul's faculty of *emunah* is especially vulnerable to certain specific *aveiros*.

Two sins in particular inflict the greatest damage on the soul's capacity for *emunah*: eating nonkosher foods and indulging in sexual immorality. If a person commits transgressions in either of these areas — if he violates the sanctity of *kedushas ha-ma'achalim* or *kedushas ha-bris* — he will weaken his capability for *emunah*. In fact, his heart could become so blocked, so

---

22. *Yoma* 39a.

heavy and opaque, that he might not even sense that there is a *Ribbono shel Olam*.

What should such a person do to recover his capacity for *emunah*? He should seek treatment. And fortunately treatments are available. Just as there are medicines for the physical heart, so too the Torah gives us medicines for the ailing spiritual heart. And they work! It may take time — rehabilitation can be a slow process — but even a heart that is heavy and sclerotic can eventually be restored to a state of supple vitality.

Rationalization

There are other processes that can interfere with the *emunah* in a Jewish heart. In a healthy individual, the natural power of *emunah* will inform and infuse the intellect, and the intellect, in turn, will direct the emotions. However, the direction of influence can also be reversed. Human nature is such that powerful emotions can influence and undermine the operation of the intellect and the conscious mind. This is the process called rationalization.

The two emotional forces that are generally responsible for rationalization are *ta'avah*, the desire for physical pleasure, and *ga'avah*, the desire to protect and enhance one's self-image. We know, for example, that our ancestors were attracted to idolatry not because of its theology, but because it provided a license for sexual immorality.[23] The beliefs associated with idolatry were secondary — just the mind's attempt to rationalize the desires of the heart.

This is why some people find it so difficult to accept the Torah's account of Creation even though it is possible to recognize the *Ribbono shel Olam* in every cubic millimeter of the world. If the Torah were only a book of cosmology, a descrip-

---

23. *Sanhedrin* 63b.

tion of the early history of the universe, these people would be willing to accept it. But the Torah continues beyond the story of Creation; it informs us that we ourselves are obligated to perform mitzvos — today. Performing mitzvos means reining in our desires in order to do what Hashem wants. That is why such people find it difficult to accept the Torah's account of Creation — not for any intellectual or epistemological reasons.

Since the Torah threatens to limit their desires, the powerful forces of *ta'avah* in the personality line up to do battle against it. They subvert the integrity of the intellect and bribe it with the illusory currency of promised pleasures. Like the corrupt judiciary in a dictatorship, the intellect learns to ignore the obvious. Its opinions are needed only to lend a mantle of respectability to decisions that have already been made by the ruling powers — the powers of *ta'avah*.

Ga'avah is also working behind the scenes to undermine the impartiality of the intellect. To some extent, consciously or unconsciously, every Jew senses the goodness, the beauty, and the sweetness — the intense desirability — of living according to the Torah. But at the same time, a Jew who is far from the Torah doubts that he could ever control the desires that now dominate him. He is convinced (albeit wrongly) that if he tried, he would fail — and nobody wants to fail.

Why should a person admit to himself that the goal is sweet and precious when he thinks it is beyond his reach? That would be frustrating, and, even worse, it would be deeply painful to his ego. It is much easier to persuade himself that the goal is not really worth the effort.

This is the process of rationalization — driven by *ga'avah*. It is like the response of the fox in the well-known parable of "The Fox and the Grapes": *It doesn't bother me that I can't reach the grapes*, the fox tells himself. *They're sour anyway.*

Thus it is not questions about *emunah* that make it difficult for some Jews to accept the Torah; it is the restrictions the Torah would impose on them. This is precisely what happened when Hashem offered the Torah to the descendants of Esav.[24] There was no doubt in their minds that it was God's Torah, but they refused it anyway, because it said that murder was prohibited. Since they weren't willing to control their desires, and they didn't think it was possible, they simply ignored the offer. What they were really saying was, "I'm sorry. It's just not my cup of tea." They didn't want to have to control their desires and eliminate their arrogance.

A Veneer of Disbelief

Thus by the process of rationalization it is possible for a Jew to ignore his instinctive knowledge of God and to commit himself to ideas that are far less compelling intellectually. On a deeper level, however, when a Jew says he does not believe, he is simply lying. He may act as if he does not believe, he may persuade others, and he may even persuade himself — but the truth is that he is making a mistake about himself. A Jew's knowledge of God is an intrinsic part of his being, and even when he conceals this knowledge from himself, it continues to exist within him.

A Jew who says he does not believe in God is called a *kofer* (כופר). To appreciate the implications of this word, we should see how it is used in other contexts. In monetary law, for example, a *kofer* is a defendant who lies about his financial obligations.[25] He himself knows the truth, but he is trying to deceive others. So too, a Jew who says he does not believe is doing his best to fool the world, but he himself knows the truth.

The root meaning of the word *kofer* is "to cover."[26] We see

---

24. *Sifrei* 343 on *Devarim* 33:2.
25. See *Baba Metzia* 3a, and *Rashi* on *Shemos* 22:8.
26. See *Rashi* on *Shemos* 25:17, s.v. *"v'asisa kapores."*

this from the word *kapores* (כפרת), which was a cover on the *Aron Kodesh*, the Holy Ark, in the *Beis Ha-Mikdash*. Even the word *kapparah* (כפרה), "atonement," is related, since through the process of atonement, sin is covered and concealed. Similarly, a Jewish *kofer* is a person who "covers up" the reality of his own being. For, in essence, he too is a believer.

The deepest implications of a word are often revealed by the way it is used in the Torah for the first time. The word *kofer* first appears when Hashem tells Noach to build the ark: וכפרת אתה מבית ומחוץ בכפר — "you shall smear it, on the inside and the outside, with a *layer of tar*."[27] Thus we discover that the word *kofer* means a thin, external coating — a veneer. In other words, a Jewish *kofer* is a person who has covered himself with a thin layer of disbelief. But if you look just beneath the surface, you will find a believer.

NURTURING FAITH — THE MITZVAH OF EMUNAH

We pointed out earlier that the mitzvah of *emunah* does not appear in the Torah in the form of an imperative statement. The Torah never commands us directly, "You shall believe in Hashem." This was difficult to understand, especially according to the Rambam, who counts *emunah* as one of the 613 mitzvos. Now, however, in the light of what we know about *emunah*, this makes perfect sense.

The Torah does not command a Jew to believe in God — because it does not have to. A Jew already believes! In his heart there is an innate and inextinguishable knowledge of God, that is an inheritance from Avraham Avinu. True, this inborn *emunah* can become weak; it can be ignored and even forgotten. But even then, it only needs to be remembered, not recreated. A Jew never needs to put *emunah* into his heart, he only

---

27. *Bereshis* 6:14.

needs to rediscover and to nurture the *emunah* that is already within him.

In other words, according to the Rambam, the mitzvah of *emunah* obligates a Jew to protect and nurture the *emunah* that is already his. As King David writes, *"Re'eh emunah,"* which means literally, "Be a shepherd to *emunah*."[28] We must take care of the *emunah* within us; we must nourish it and guard it with all the watchfulness and diligence of a shepherd tending his sheep.

Just as we are obligated to care for the physical body by giving it nutritious food, so too we must care for the soul and its power of *emunah* by giving it a healthy spiritual diet. This means learning Torah and performing mitzvos, for these are the "foods" that strengthen the power of *emunah* and keep it healthy.

The mitzvah of *emunah* also obligates us to avoid anything that might damage the soul's capacity for *emunah*. Since every *aveirah* weakens this capacity, the mitzvah of *emunah* imposes an additional obligation to avoid *aveiros*, and especially the two *aveiros* most detrimental to *emunah* — forbidden foods and sexual immorality.

Aveiros cause damage to *emunah* indirectly. They weaken the powers of the soul in general, and thus, the power of *emunah* is also weakened. But some threats to *emunah* are more direct — such as exposing oneself to *apikorsus*, the ideas and doctrines of disbelief. To do so is the spiritual equivalent of entering a room that is contaminated by the germs of an infectious disease. Whether or not a person will be harmed by such an exposure may depend on the strength of his immune system and his general state of health. But just as we are commanded to maintain the well-being of our souls in a general

---

28. *Tehillim* 37:3.

way by doing mitzvos and avoiding *aveiros*, we are also commanded to avoid unnecessary spiritual risks.

A PEOPLE DEFINED BY FAITH

A Jew who is spiritually healthy believes instinctively in Hashem, and the first person with this kind of belief was Avraham Avinu. We mention this fact every morning in the section of our prayers known as *Pesukei d'Zimrah*:

אתה הוא ד' לבדך	*You alone are God.*
את עשית את השמים	*You made the heavens,*
שמי השמים	*The heavens above the heavens*
וכל צבאם	*and all the angels,*
הארץ וכל אשר עליה	*the earth and all that is upon it,*
הימים וכל אשר בהם	*the oceans and all that is within them.*
ואתה מחיה את כלם	*You provide them all with life,*
וצבא השמים	*and the angels of Heaven*
לך משתחוים.	*bow to You in obedience.*[29]

In this verse we praise God as the author and artist of Creation. We contemplate the grandeur of His handiwork — the majestic sweep of the heavenly spaces and the angelic armies in their glorious array. We consider the vast oceans brimming with life and the solid soil of the earth, home to all the creatures of the land.

And yet, for all its grandeur, the world described in this verse is incomplete. The fish and the birds, the stars and the planets, are all in place, but there is one essential ingedient missing: a human being who will recognize and serve the Creator. Only when the world contains a person who believes in the *Ribbono shel Olam* can it be complete. Only with the arrival of Avraham Avinu does the work of Creation reach its goal —

---

29. *Nechemiah* 9:6.

and that is what we say, in a verse whose opening words parallel those of the previous one:

אתה הוא ד' האלקים	*You are Hashem, the God*
אשר בחרת באברם	*Who chose Avram*
והוצאתו מאור כשדים	*and brought him out of Ur Kasdim*
ושמת שמו	*and You gave him the name*
אברהם.	*Avraham.*[30]

This verse emphasizes that Hashem changed Avraham's name: first he was *Avram*, and then he became *Avraham*. Why of all the things we could say about Avraham do we mention this? Why indeed was it even necessary for Hashem to change his name?

A New Power of Procreation

The Torah tells us that Avraham and Sarah were unable to have children for many years. Then, in their old age, after decades of prayer and waiting, Hashem performed a miracle for them, and they were blessed with a child.[31] But why did Avraham and Sarah need an act of Divine intervention in order to have children?

The answer to this question is based on an idea we have already mentioned: Avraham and Sarah were the prototypes of a new species. Every existing species has the power to reproduce itself, and each new member of the species inherits that power from its parents, together with all the other traits and abilities of the species. But Avraham and Sarah were the first members of a new species, not a continuation of the human race that had started with Adam.

The link between generations had been broken. Any child

---

30. Ibid., 7.
31. *Bereshis*, ch.15-18.

born to Avraham and Sarah would be essentially different from the children of earlier generations; he would belong to a new species. Hence the power to bring that child into the world was not something Avraham and Sarah could have inherited from their own parents.

Thus the miracle that enabled Avraham and Sarah to become the father and the mother of the Jewish people was by no means incidental. The Jewish nation had to begin that way. A new species was about to begin, and therefore Hashem had to provide Avraham and Sarah with a new power of procreation.

In fact, that new power was given to Avraham at the moment when the letter *heh* was added to his name: "You will no longer be called Avram (אברם), but your name will be Avraham (אברהם), for I have made you a father of many nations."[32]

Logically, there are two ways one could understand this change of name: as a result or a cause. One could suggest that Hashem gave Avraham a new power of procreation, and He also gave him the new name to reflect this change. Here the name is a result. Alternatively, one could suggest that *because* Avraham received a new name, it became possible for him to receive a new power of procreation from Hashem. Here the name is a cause. The second approach is the correct one. This is clear from a comment in the Zohar[33] regarding the names of Yaakov's four wives: Rachel (רחל), Leah (לאה), Bilhah (בלהה), and Zilpah (זלפה). Each of these names includes the letter *heh*, except for Rachel. In the name of Bilhah, however, there are two *heh*s. The Midrash explains that one of them was for Bilhah herself, while the second was for Rachel, so that she too would be able to bear children. Thus we see that the letter *heh* not only symbolized the power of procreation, but also, in some way,

32. Ibid. 17:5.
33. *Zohar Chadash, Behar*, s.v. *LeHanchil ohavei yesh*.

carried and conferred this power.[34]

Why was it specifically the letter *heh* that bestowed the power of procreation? Here the grammar of *lashon ha-kodesh* provides an insight. In Hebrew, a *heh* at the end of a word usually indicates a feminine noun or adjective. The letter *heh*, in other words, is a "feminine letter." Since the power of childbirth is a feminine power, it is logical for it to be associated with the feminine letter, *heh*.

Thus with the gift of the letter *heh*, Avraham received the power to perpetuate a new species, and that was the moment when the Jewish people really came into existence. The next verse in *Pesukei d'Zimrah* directs our attention to the defining characteristic of this new species of humanity:

ומצאת את לבבו   *You found his heart*

נאמן לפניך.... *faithful before You....*[35]

As we have said, Avraham Avinu was different because of his belief in Hashem. His heart is *ne'eman*; it is full of *emunah*. He has a heart that is charged with faith, and he imbued his descendants with this same faith. That is the essential point which makes them different. Their faith is so deep within them and such an essential part of their being that it can be transmitted by inheritance. The defining characteristic of the new species is *emunah*, a hereditary knowledge of God.

"You found his heart faithful before You" — You created a new species with a faithful heart, a heart that contains *emunah*.

---

34. The name of any created being in *lashon ha-kodesh* is related to the essence of that being. In fact, according to the Kabbalists, the letters of a name in *lashon ha-kodesh* are actually the channels through which that particular being receives the Divine energy that is the source of its existence and life at every moment.
35. *Nechemiah* 9:8.

Exempt from Filial Obligation

With this, we can also understand an aspect of Avraham's life that might otherwise seem puzzling. When Avraham received the command to leave his home and to set out on his journey to Eretz Yisrael, he was accompanied by his wife, Sarah, his nephew Lot, and a large entourage of disciples and servants — but *not* by his father, Terach.[36] Terach, who was then one hundred and forty-five years old, was left behind in Charan. But how could Avraham abandon his elderly father? Why did he ignore the mitzvah of *kibbud av*, the mitzvah to care for a parent?

The Midrash explains that Hashem told Avraham, "You are exempt from the mitzvah of honoring your father. No one else in the world is exempt from this mitzvah."[37] Avraham was unique in this respect. The mitzvah of *kibbud av* did not apply to him. And the reason was that Avraham was the first member of a new species. Avraham was not a continuation, or even an improvement, of what Terach was. He was not obligated to show *kibbud av* for Terach because in the deepest sense Terach was not his father. Avraham was the first link of a new chain, a new beginning, and that was also why Avraham was commanded to travel to Eretz Yisrael.

ERETZ YISRAEL: THE LAND OF ALL BEGINNINGS

Each of the first three portions of the Torah contains a story of creation. In *Bereshis*, we witness the creation of the world. In *Noach*, we see the creation of a new world after the flood — Noach's world. And then, in *Lech Lecha*, we read of the creation of yet another world — the Jewish world. It is a new and essentially different world, because it now includes the Jewish

---

36. See *Rashi* on *Bereshis* 11:32.
37. *Bereshis Rabbah* 39:8.

people, who are the purpose of Creation.

Lech Lecha begins with the words "Hashem said to Avram, 'Go from your country....'"[38] This was the first time God revealed Himself to Avraham, and the very first thing He told him was, "Go to the Land of Israel." As the first Jew, Avraham was the beginning of a new species and the seed of a new world — and that is why Hashem told him to go to Eretz Yisrael. Eretz Yisrael is the first land, the place with which the creation of the world began, and hence it has a deep connection with other "firsts." Indeed, when we look carefully in the Torah itself, we discover that at every significant starting point, at every moment of beginning, there is an allusion to Eretz Yisrael.

The First Verse

The very first verse of the Torah hints at Eretz Yisrael. בראשית ברא אלקים means "In the beginning of God's creation," and the creation of the world began with Eretz Yisrael. In the words of our Sages: "The Land of Israel was created at the beginning, and all the [rest of the] world was created at the end."[39]

The first piece of the physical world that Hashem created was the *even shesiyah*, the "foundation stone,"[40] which eventually became the location of the *Kodesh Ha-Kodashim*, the Holy of Holies, in the *Beis Ha-Mikdash*. This primordial object of creation functioned as a kind of embryo for the earth. From it the entire world developed — first Yerushalayim, then the Land of Israel, and finally all the other parts of the globe.

The First Word

Even the very first word of the Torah contains an allusion to

---

38. *Bereshis* 12:1.
39. *Ta'anis* 10a.
40. *Bemidbar Rabbah* 12:4.

Eretz Yisrael. The Gemara tells us that the Hebrew word *bereshis* (בראשית) can be read as two words: *bara shis* (ברא שית), a phrase that means, "He created the *shissin*."[41] The *shissin* were deep, subterranean channels under the courtyard of the *Beis Ha-Mikdash* through which wine poured on the altar could flow into the earth. Thus the very first word of the Torah alludes to a place in Eretz Yisrael, namely, the site of the altar in the courtyard of the Holy Temple.

The First Man

This site is connected with yet another beginning: that of all mankind. Human history begins with Adam Ha-Rishon in the Garden of Eden, but if we search for the origin of Adam himself, we come back to the site of the altar. *Chazal* tell us that when God took a piece of earth in order to make a body for Adam Ha-Rishon, He took it from this spot.[42] Thus Adam Ha-Rishon, and all humanity, have their beginning in Eretz Yisrael.

The connection is even deeper than location. Adam Ha-Rishon was not only created *in* Eretz Yisrael; he was created *from* Eretz Yisrael, from a physical piece of Eretz Yisrael. Thus the beginning of all mankind — in a very literal and concrete sense — is Eretz Yisrael.

The First Topic

Even the reason why the Torah begins with an account of the creation of the world is related to Eretz Yisrael. The Torah's real purpose in telling the story of Creation is not to give us a glimpse into the secrets of the Creator. Rather, it is to provide us with a logically unassailable argument that Eretz Yisrael belongs to the Jewish people.

---

41. *Sukkah* 49a.
42. *Yerushalmi, Nazir* 7:2.

That is what Rashi explains in the first few lines of his commentary on the *Chumash*.[43] The Torah begins with the story of Creation because one day the nations of the world may accuse the Jewish people of acquiring the Land of Israel unjustly. "You are robbers," they will say, "because you conquered Eretz Yisrael from the seven nations who lived there."

When that happens, Rashi continues, we should refer our critics to what is written in the Torah and reply, " The entire world belongs to God, because He created it. That is what we learn from *parashas Bereshis*. Hence God has the right to give Eretz Yisrael to whomever He chooses. It was His decision that the seven nations should live there for a time, and it was His decision to take it away fom them and to give it to us. This is also clearly stated by the Torah in many places."

The First Haftarah

The first *haftarah* of the year, which we read on the Shabbos of *parashas Bereshis*, also begins with an allusion to Eretz Yisrael:

כה אמר הקל ד'	*Thus says God, Hashem,*
בורא השמים	*Who created the heavens*
ונוטיהם	*and set them in their place,*
רקע הארץ	*Who spread out the land*
וצאצאיה	*and all that it brought forth,*
נתן נשמה	*Who gives a soul*
לעם עליה	*to the people who are upon it*
ורוח	*and a spirit*
להלכים בה.	*to those who walk within it.*[44]

Which land is being described here? Which land gives a soul to the people who live upon it? The Gemara's answer is

---

43. *Rashi* on *Bereshis* 1:1, s.v. "bereshis."
44. *Yeshayahu* 42:5.

Eretz Yisrael.[45] And from the phrase that begins "Who gives a soul to the people who are upon it," we learn that a person who lives in Eretz Yisrael will be forgiven for his sins and will receive the reward of *Olam Ha-Ba*, the World to Come. Even one who merely walks four cubits in Eretz Yisrael will receive a share in the World to Come.[46] Thus the verse *Chazal* chose for our annual introduction to the Prophets also speaks about Eretz Yisrael.

First Words to the Avos

Eretz Yisrael is also connected to another important set of beginnings. When Hashem revealed Himself to each one of the *Avos*, His very first words were about Eretz Yisrael. To Avraham He said, "Go out from your land...to the land I will show you,"[47] and that new land, of course, was Eretz Yisrael. Similarly, the first thing Hashem told Yitzchak was, "Do not go down to Egypt," but rather, "Dwell in this land...."[48] Thus, for both Avraham and Yitzchak, the experience of Divine revelation began with a command to live in Eretz Yisrael.

If we look carefully, however, we notice a difference between the way Hashem spoke to Avraham and the way He spoke to Yitzchak, and this reflects a fundamental difference in the way each of them served Hashem. Avraham Avinu personified the attribute of *chessed*, the spiritual power that leads to the emotion of love and to deeds of kindness. Through his love for God and his fellow man, Avraham perfected the trait of *chessed* as a way of serving God, and he bequeathed this trait to his descendants. If today we have any love for the *Ribbono shel Olam*, it is because we inherit it from Avraham Avinu.

---

45. *Kesubos* 111a.
46. Ibid.
47. *Bereshis* 12:1.
48. Ibid. 26:2.

The performance of a positive mitzvah, a commandment that requires us to perform an action, brings us closer to God. Hence, our desire to perform such a mitzvah is an expression of our love for God. Since the trait of *chessed* is the source of our love for God, it is also the source of our motivation to perform the positive commandments. That is why Avraham Avinu, who personified *chessed*, was given the mitzvah of settling in Eretz Yisrael as a positive commandment — "Go to Eretz Yisrael."

Yitzchak, on the other hand, personified the attribute of *din*, the spiritual power that leads to the emotion of fear and restrains a person from acting with the indiscriminate kindness of *chessed*. It is in relation to Yitzchak that God is called: *Pachad Yitzchak*, "the Fear of Yitzchak," and Yitzchak, through his *avodah* and self-sacrifice, perfected the trait of *din* as a way of serving God.

The attribute of *din* advises a person to refrain from giving unless the recipient is truly deserving, and so it is expressed in the personality as the quality of self-restraint. Since it holds a person back from action, the attribute of *din* is the source of our determination to observe the prohibitions of the Torah. We refrain from committing a sin because we fear Hashem, because we are in awe of His greatness, and because we are afraid to do anything that would separate us from Him. That is why Yitzchak, who personified the attribute of *din*, was given the mitzvah of Eretz Yisrael in the form of a prohibition: "Do not go down to Egypt," or in other words, "Do not leave Eretz Yisrael."

When Yaakov Avinu experienced prophecy for the first time, we also find that Hashem spoke to him about Eretz Yisrael. As Yaakov lay sleeping and dreaming on Mount Moriah, Hashem told him:

אני ד׳   *I am Hashem,*

אלקי אברהם אביך   *the God of Avraham your father*

ואלקי יצחק   *and the God of Yitzchak.*

הארץ אשר אתה שכב עליה   *The land on which you are lying*

לך אתננה   *I will give to you*

ולזרעך   *and to your descendants.*[49]

The First Person Belongs in the First Land

Thus Eretz Yisrael is the first land, and the land of all that is first. It is a land linked to all beginnings, and that is why, at every starting point in the Torah, we discover Eretz Yisrael.

There is one first land — Eretz Yisrael. And there is one first person — Avraham Avinu. Avraham was the first person to serve Hashem with *emunah*. He was the first Jew, the first member of a new species endowed with a hereditary knowledge of God. Avraham was the purpose and the goal of Creation, and the person of *bereshis* belongs in the land of *bereshis*. The first person belongs in the first land, and that is what we learn from the first verse of *Lech Lecha*.

---

49. Ibid. 28:13.

2.

THE PURIFICATION OF FAITH

THE AKEIDAH

Avraham Avinu, the father of the Jewish people, faced ten *nisyonos* in his lifetime, ten tests of faith.[1] The last and most difficult one was the Divine command to sacrifice Yitzchak, his beloved son. It was the test that clearly demonstrated the power and purity of Avraham's faith for all generations to come. But what exactly was this test we call "the *akeidah*"?

We usually assume that the *akeidah* proved Avraham's willingness to sacrifice his son in obedience to God's command. This characterization, however, does not stand up to scrutiny. Avraham *was*, of course, willing to sacrifice Yitzchak. But in light of what we know about Avraham, that would not have been the ultimate challenge. Avraham had already proven, on many occasions, that he was willing to give up anything and everything for God.

THE FIRST TEST

Consider what we know about Avraham Avinu. He had grown up in Ur Kasdim, a city steeped in *avodah zarah*, idolatry. His parents and neighbors worshiped the stars and

---

1. *Avos* 5:3.

bowed to idols. But when Avraham was only three years old, he began to search for the truth. With no teacher or tradition, he was guided only by his own profound intellect and his unswerving passion for truth. Nevertheless, he recognized the fundamental error of *avodah zarah*.

Avraham came to realize that there is one God who created the entire universe and continues to sustain it. He understood that God directs the heavenly spheres and that there is no other God. The Rambam notes that by the age of forty, Avraham had attained a clear recognition of the Creator.[2]

From that time on, Avraham set a course for himself that was determined solely and uncompromisingly by his understanding of God. Alone and unafraid, he set out to convince the world of the error of *avodah zarah* — an error that had gradually turned people's minds away from their Creator. Undeterred by danger, Avraham openly proclaimed that all worship must be directed to God. He taught that graven images and idols must be destroyed. Privately and publicly, he admonished and persuaded, argued and debated, and when it began to be clear that his arguments were irrefutable, he was arrested.

Even when he was taken prisoner and brought before the tyrant Nimrod, compromise was unthinkable. All that mattered to Avraham was the truth, and the task of teaching the truth. The Midrash describes how Avraham spoke with Nimrod — calmly, humorously, and patiently — as if he were trying to bring Nimrod to see for himself the absurdity of worshiping a created being.

"You are mocking me!" shouted Nimrod, who worshiped fire. "So let your invisible God come and save you from my fire!" With that, he ordered his servants to throw Avraham into a blazing furnace.

---

2. *Mishneh Torah, Hilchos Avodas Kochavim* 1:3.

A stunning and unexpected miracle took place. Avraham emerged from the furnace unharmed. But the miracle had been completely unanticipated — Avraham had expected to die for his faith *al kiddush Hashem,* sanctifying God's Name.[3]

That was only the first of the ten tests Avraham would eventually undergo. Yet we see that even then, many years before the *akeidah,* Avraham was willing to sacrifice everything for God.

In some ways, that first test seems an even greater demonstration of faith than the *akeidah.* At the *akeidah,* Hashem spoke to Avraham directly and told him what to do. By that time, Avraham was already familiar with the voice of prophecy, and God had spoken to him many times.

In Ur Kasdim, however, Avraham was forced to act on his own. He had discovered God, but God had not yet spoken to him. Avraham knew about God, but his knowledge was the product of intellect and logic. He had not yet experienced God as the living, transcendent reality Who would later reveal Himself through prophecy. Hashem first spoke to Avraham directly with the command of *"Lech lecha,"* which was after his confrontation with Nimrod. And yet, in Ur Kasdim, even without the experience of prophecy, Avraham's belief was so strong that he was willing to sacrifice his life for God.

Furthermore, at the time of the first test in Ur Kasdim, Avraham was utterly alone. He was one individual against an entire civilization. He and his beliefs were targets of public ridicule and organized persecution. In contrast, when the *akeidah* took place, Avraham was widely recognized as a great spiritual leader, and even monarchs regarded him with reverence and fear.

In this light, then, the episode in Ur Kasdim appears to have been a more difficult trial and a greater proof of faith than

---

3. *Bereshis Rabbah* 38:8.

the *akeidah*. But this is contradicted not only by the words of our Sages, but by logic as well. To see why this is logically untenable, we must understand the reason why God tests man at all.

AN UPWARD PROMOTION

The word *nisayon* in Hebrew has two meanings. The first is "test" or "trial." We are presented with a challenge. When we overcome it, we demonstrate that we possess a certain quality or ability.

The word *nisayon* also connotes "elevation," as we see from Moshe Rabbeinu's use of the term. At Mount Sinai, Moshe explained to the Jewish people why Hashem revealed Himself to them amid thunderous sounds and fiery visions: *"l'va'avur nasos eschem,"*[4] which Rashi translates, "in order to make you great." The word *nasos*, Rashi explains, is related to the word *nes*, a banner raised up high.

Actually, both these meanings — "test" and "elevation" — are just two aspects of the same thing. The purpose of a test is to raise a person to a higher level. In school, for example, before a student advances to a higher grade, he takes a test. When he passes, he can be promoted. So too, when Hashem gives a *nisayon*, it is in order to raise a person to a new and higher spiritual level.

Avraham Avinu underwent a long series of tests. Each new test raised him to a higher level, and thus each *nisayon* had to be more challenging than the previous ones. If so, the last test, the *akeidah*, had to have been more difficult than the first one in Ur Kasdim.

Clearly, we have yet to identify the real challenge of the *akeidah*.

---

4. *Shemos* 20:17.

THE CONTRADICTION

The key to understanding the *akeidah* is provided by the *Zohar haKadosh*.[5] The greatness of Avraham Avinu at the *akeidah* was not his willingness to sacrifice his son Yitzchak. As we have explained, that would not have been the ultimate test. Rather, the real challenge stemmed from the promise Hashem had made earlier: "Through Yitzchak you will have offspring."[6] Avraham's descendants, his physical and spiritual heirs, were to come from Yitzchak. This clearly implied that Yitzchak himself was destined to father a son, a Yaakov.

But then Hashem commanded Avraham to offer Yitzchak as a sacrifice. Suddenly Hashem appeared to be breaking His promise, rescinding His commitment, and this too seemed clear and undeniable. Yet, at the same time, Avraham knew, with absolute certainty, that Hashem neither lies nor breaks His promises.

Thus, Avraham found himself confronted by two contradictory truths. On the one hand, he had received a Divine promise of a future that would spring from his son Yitzchak. On the other, he had received a direct command from God to destroy that future — forever. And so these two truths began to battle within Avraham. Each truth by itself was undeniable; together they were utterly incompatible.

As we have explained, the command to sacrifice Yitzchak, by itself, was not the ultimate test for Avraham. He had long ago set aside any personal considerations, and his only desire was to fulfill the will of God as he knew it through prophecy. But to discover that within the will of God itself, within the very words Hashem had spoken to him, there was a terrible contradiction — this was incomprehensible!

---

5. *Zohar* I:120a.
6. *Bereshis* 21:12.

This was a challenge that shook the very foundations of his being, for it threatened to drive a wedge between himself and his Maker. Avraham had discovered God through the power of his own intellect, but now God had become baffling and obscure. Avraham had been attached to God with every fiber of his being, but now he felt as if God had become distant and unapproachable.

As the *Zohar* explains,[7] this insight is contained in the Torah's description of the journey to Mount Moriah: "*Va-yar es ha-makom me-rachok.* — He [Avraham] saw the place from afar."[8] The word *ha-makom* is often used as a name for Hashem Himself, and so the verse can be understood to mean "He saw Hashem from afar." For the first time, Hashem appeared distant from him. The close relationship with God that Avraham had forged seemed to be in jeopardy. This verse has the same meaning, the *Zohar* says, as the verse "*Me-rachok Hashem nireh li* — From afar Hashem appeared to me."[9]

This was a terrible *nisayon* even for Avraham Avinu. But not only for Avraham! There is simply no greater *nisayon* than that of a Jew who finds himself baffled by contradictions, assailed by questions, and tormented by doubts about God.

---

7. *Ad loc.*

8. *Bereshis* 22:4.

9. *Yirmeyahu* 31:2. The *Zohar* here also suggests a second interpretation of the word *ha-Makom*: that it refers to Yaakov. Both interpretations, however, are saying essentially the same thing. If Avraham were to sacrifice Yitzchak, then according to logic, Yaakov could not be born. Thus it seemed to Avraham that the possibility of having a Yaakov was becoming distant (second interpretation). And since that would contradict Hashem's promise, Avraham also felt that Hashem was becoming distant (first interpretation). Hence the verse has the same meaning as "*me-rachok Hashem nireh li.*"

THE RESPONSE OF FAITH

When Avraham found himself bewildered by an unresolvable contradiction, when he realized that he could not understand, he did not relinquish either belief or hope. On the contrary, his response was to strengthen himself with *emunah peshutah*, with a faith that was simple, pure, and unconditional. Although he had no answers, he refused to question. Although he was perplexed, he refused to doubt. Indeed, there was a paradox, but then again, God had never told him he was expected to understand everything. What *was* clear, however, was that God had commanded him to bring his son Yitzchak as a sacrifice, and so Avraham proceeded to do exactly that — with alacrity, determination, and joy. And *that* was the true greatness of Avraham Avinu at the *akeidah*.

In retrospect, we know that there never was a contradiction. The conflict between God's promise of a future for Avraham and His command to destroy it was only apparent. There was a remarkably simple way to reconcile the two statements — an answer so simple that even a young child in *cheder* can explain it. But this answer was revealed to Avraham only after he had successfully completed the *nisayon*. In the midst of the ordeal, the contradiction was terribly real.

In the midst of the *nisayon*, baffled by contradiction, Avraham had to travel with Yitzchak to Mount Moriah. In a world that seemed suddenly bereft of logic, he had to bind Yitzchak and place him on the altar. For the sake of a God who had become distant and unknowable, Avraham had to force his hand to pick up the knife.

Then, at the last moment, an angel called out the Divine command from Heaven: "Avraham, Avraham...do not harm the boy...for now I know that you fear God...."[10] At that point,

---

10. *Bereshis* 22:12.

the *nisayon* was over — and only then was the contradiction explained to Avraham, as Rashi relates[11] in his account of the following dialogue: "Now I will reveal my thoughts to You," Avraham said to Hashem. "First You told me, 'You will have descendants from Yitzchak.' But then You commanded me, 'Take your son Yitzchak for a sacrifice....' And finally You told me, 'Do not harm the boy.' "

Avraham, of course, was speaking without anger or complaint. One who listens carefully can hear that Avraham, always the humble and obedient servant, was pleading with God for enlightenment: "See the confusion and darkness in which Your servant waits," he was saying. "I only ask to know Your will so that I may fulfill it."

Hashem answered him, "Although that is the way it appeared to you, it was not really so. In truth, I never changed My mind. My words are never false, and My promises are always fulfilled. I never told you to *slaughter* Yitzchak, only to *take him up* as a sacrifice, to place him on the altar. And now that you have taken him up, I am telling you to bring him down."

THE NATURE OF A NISAYON

But if the answer was so simple and obvious, why did it have to be revealed by an angel? Why wasn't Avraham able to think of it himself?

The question is astonishing when we consider the power of Avraham's mind. On his own, he had extricated himself from the philosophical errors of an entire civilization. He had solved the riddle of an opaque world, looking beneath the veil of creation to discover the Creator. For Avraham, the entire physical world was a transparent metaphor, an open declaration of God.

---

11. *Rashi* on *Bereshis* 22:12, s.v. *"ki atah yadati."*

In addition, Avraham knew the entire Torah before it was given at Mount Sinai. No one had to teach it to him because he was able to find the knowledge within himself. In the language of *Chazal*, "his internal organs provided him with Godly wisdom."[12]

So how can it be that Avraham was baffled by an apparent contradiction that even a child in *cheder* can explain? Because *that* is the very nature of a *nisayon*, especially a *nisayon* in *emunah*. In a test of faith, even the obvious answers simply do not come to a person's mind.

The *nisayon* to which Avraham was subjected was the result of a Heavenly decree. The first thing the Torah tells us about the *akeidah* is "God tested Avraham."[13] The *nisayon*, in other words, was imposed from Above, and it consisted of two elements: Avraham found himself confronted by an apparently unresolvable contradiction in God's words, and, at the same time, he was commanded to commit an irrevocable act that seemed certain to destroy everything he had accomplished in a lifetime of obedience to God's will. Both elements of the test were essential, and both were the result of a Divine decree.

Thus, Avraham's inability to resolve the contradiction was imposed on him from Above. It was the Divine act of concealment that made the *nisayon* possible; it was the darkness and confusion that provided a stage upon which the test could take place. And on that dark stage, Avraham was faced with the choice of whether or not he would continue to serve God with obedience, faith, and joy.

---

12. *Avos D'Rabbi Nasan* 32:1.
13. *Bereshis* 22:1.

TESTS OF EMUNAH

So it is with all *nisyonos* in *emunah*, with all the doubts and questions about faith that can trouble a person. The questions themselves are based on the way things seem, not the way they really are. The truth is that they can be answered easily. Nevertheless, some people suffer terribly from such questions, and they are unable to accept even the most reasonable answers.

Why is this? It is because it has been decreed in Heaven that they must undergo a *nisayon* in *emunah*, and by that very decree their minds are closed and their hearts are blocked. Their inability to understand — their spiritual and intellectual blindness — that is the *nisayon* which has been imposed upon them.

Indeed, it is the most difficult *nisayon* a person can undergo — the feeling that God has hidden His face, the terrible ordeal of being unable to find God, the agonizing experience of *hester panim*. In the midst of such a *nisayon*, a person finds no joy in studying Torah, no comfort in prayer. He is unable to feel that God is watching over him and caring for him. He feels alone and abandoned, as if God had moved far away. It is the very situation which the Torah describes with the words *"Va-yar es ha-Makom me-rachok* — He saw Hashem from afar."

Such was the *nisayon* Avraham faced at the *akeidah*, and such was the *nisayon* he overcame. Avraham continued to do the will of the Creator even when his heart was heavy with questions, even when his mind was clouded and the light of faith was dim.

One reason why Avraham succeeded was that he recognized his enemy clearly. He understood the true source of the thoughts that were troubling him and the real nature of the confrontation. Within the rational arguments of his own mind, concealed within the images and impulses of his heart,

Avraham recognized the adversary, the *Satan* — the same opponent he had been battling for a lifetime. And once Avraham knew where the attack was coming from, he was able to repel it. Having unmasked the enemy, Avraham confronted him directly:[14]

> This is not the first time you have spoken. You have a long record with me. From the beginning, you have been a shameless liar, an unrepentant swindler, a continual source of disinformation, and a master of deceit. You are a crook who has been caught and convicted, time and time again, Therefore, I will not pay the slightest attention to anything you say. I will not be deterred by your arguments, and I certainly will not cast off the yoke of mitzvos by which I am bound to my Creator.
>
> I will continue to serve God to the best of my ability even now when I am groping in the darkness, bereft of understanding, abandoned by the light. The army of questions you hurl against me, the sea of sophistry with which you would sweep me away — none of these will cause me even a moment's doubt. I will continue to walk on the path of *emunah* I have chosen for myself.
>
> I also believe with perfect faith that just as it was decreed by God that now I must suffer beneath these towering waves of darkness and confusion, so too He has already appointed a time for my redemption, a precise moment when all these troubles will disappear.
>
> When that moment arrives, a brilliant light will burst forth, and I will walk again in the sunshine of a clear and luminous *emunah*. In the warmth of that light, all the questions and objections you set before me will melt away like snow in the springtime. They will vanish into the air like a morning mist.

---

14. Based on *Bereshis Rabbah*, 56:5, and *Sanhedrin* 89b.

When that moment arrives, I shall rejoice in Hashem and take pleasure in His goodness. At that time, I will reap a reward for all the afflictions and the trials I endured. Then I will delight in God's Torah, and His mitzvos will be the beloved treasure of my heart.

A SIGN FOR THE FUTURE

The *nisayon* we have just described in all its vivid details is not ancient history. It is nothing less than the *nisayon* that has descended upon the Jewish people in our own times. And this should not surprise us, since we know that everything that happened in the lives of our Patriarchs is an indication of what would happen later to their descendants, to *klal Yisrael*.[15]

The *Avos* are the root and the source of *klal Yisrael*, and the pattern of their lives is repeated in the lives of their descendants. This occurs on two levels: on a national level, in events affecting millions of people, and also on an individual level, in the life of every Jew. Thus the trials of Avraham Avinu correspond to the trials that would later confront the Jewish people in the course of their national history, and they also reflect the trials that occur in the life of every Jew.

As we have said, the final test for Avraham was the experience of *hester panim*, a condition in which belief itself seemed to become cloudy and incomprehensible, and the principles of faith were under attack. Hence we can infer that the final test for *klal Yisrael*, in the period just before the arrival of Mashiach, will be very much the same.

And, indeed, that is precisely the situation today. The entire world is full of doubts about Hashem. Secular culture, from the streets to the universities, is a culture of disbelief, and the mass media broadcast their voices of scorn and derision to ev-

---

15. כל מה שאירע לאבות סימן לבנים — *Ramban* on *Bereshis* 12:6.

ery corner of the globe.

Even among our own people, there are Jews who have become the spokesmen for disbelief. Having casually abandoned the restraints of tradition and Jewish law, these individuals feel free to hurl unrighteous accusations against faith and against God Himself. They assure themselves that they are motivated by a great love for *klal Yisrael*. "How can we be silent," these self-appointed defenders of the Jewish people proclaim, "when God has abandoned His nation, and our people has suffered such terrible tragedies?" And so they mount their vehement attacks against faith under the banner of a self-made righteousness — a righteousness defined by their own capricious minds and driven by the fickle winds of intellectual fashion.

In such a generation, fortunate are the faithful — those with a pure heart who justify the ways of God. For the test of *emunah* is the principal *nisayon* of our generation. It is, in fact, the very reason why we have come into the world.

The sages of the last few generations agree that we have already entered the period of history called *"ikvesa d'Meshicha"* — the era preceding the arrival of Mashiach. It is clear from the statements of *Chazal* and from the prophecies at the end of the book of *Daniel* that the most formidable tests of faith will occur in this final act of human history. Later sources[16] tell us that in the period just before the final redemption, "a flood of heresy will descend upon the world" and mankind will be inundated by disbelief and immorality.

This is how the Mishnah described it some two thousand years ago: "In the era before the arrival of Mashiach, the government will become one of heresy."[17] Elsewhere, the Gemara

---

16. See, for example, *V'Hilchosa K'Nachmani*, p. 20, section 16.
17. *Sotah* 9:15.

describes the same phenomenon: "Before Mashiach arrives, the entire government will turn into one of heresy."[18]

As always, the words of our Sages are true on a number of levels. When the Gemara refers to "a goverment of heresy" it is speaking not only about politics, but also about spiritual forces in the lives of individuals.

There is a parallel between the world at large and the private, inner world of each individual. "Every man is a miniature world,"[19] a microcosm in which the entire universe is reflected.

Hence, in a generation like our own, when the rule of heresy is threatening to extend its power in the external, physical world, every individual needs to guard his inner, spiritual world with extraordinary vigilance. He must defend himself with tenacity and determination so that the "government of heresy" led by "the old and foolish king"[20] — the *yetzer ha-ra* — will not succeed in extending its power within the miniature world of his own mind and body.

WHEN A "HEEL" LISTENS

The name that *Chazal* chose for our generation gives us an insight into our place in history. *Ikvesa d'Meshicha* literally means "on the heels of Mashiach." On the simplest level it means that we are only a few steps away from the time when Mashiach will arrive. But there is a deeper reason for this particular expression.

Our tradition tells us that the Jewish souls of all the generations constitute a single spiritual entity with a structure comparable to the human body. This collective entity corresponds to the body of the first man, Adam Ha-Rishon.[21] The souls of

---

18. *Sanhedrin* 97a.
19. *Tikkunei Zohar* 130b (Zhitomir, Slavita).
20. See *Rashi* on *Koheles* 4:13.

the earliest generations correspond to and are derived from the highest part of Adam's body — his head. In contrast, the souls of the last generations, in the era before Mashiach, come from the lowest part of Adam's body — his heels. Hence today, in the period of *ikvesa d'Meshicha*, the souls of our generation are derived from the heels of Adam Ha-Rishon. That is why *Chazal* chose this name to describe us.

In what way do the souls of our generation resemble heels? No other part of the body is so distant from the head, and no other part of the body is so numb, so tough, and so lacking in sensitivity. Not only is the heel incapable of thinking thoughts and feeling emotions, as the head does, but the heel can barely even feel what is happening within its own flesh. Even if the callused skin of the heel is stabbed with a needle, there is almost no sensation of pain.

So it is with our own generation. Never in history has there been a generation so lacking in feeling and sensitivity for Godliness. Never has there been a generation so numb to its own injuries, so unconcerned about the damage that is being done to it. In our own time, millions of souls have been torn away from the Jewish people, and yet the pain of that loss is hardly felt — for it is a generation of insensitivity.

And yet, precisely because the souls of our generation are so poorly endowed, our own meager spiritual accomplishments are of tremendous significance to God. It is not only that every mitzvah is more difficult today or that spirituality itself is a rare commodity for which one must pay dearly. It is also because the contribution every mitzvah makes to the world today is vastly more important. In a time of darkness, even the smallest light is precious. In a generation of numb and calloused souls, even the simple faith of an ordinary Jew is a cause

---

21. See *Tanya, Iggeres Ha-Kodesh*, p. 111b.

for immeasurable delight in Heaven.

This is the message Rav Mordechai of Lechovitch[22] finds in the verse *"V'hayah ekev tishme'un,"* which is usually translated, "It shall be, because you listen..."[23] *Chazal,* however, tell us that the word *v'hayah* is an indication of joy,[24] and in the word *ekev* we recognize an allusion to *ikvesa d'Meshicha,* the generation at the end of history.

Hence, the Lechovitcher Rav interprets these words as saying that there will be great joy in Heaven when a "heel" listens, when the lowly souls of *ikvesa d'Meshicha* obey God's commandments.[25]

We find a similar idea in Hashem's promise to Avraham immediately following the *akeidah:* "Since you have done this...I will bless you greatly.... All the nations of the world will be blessed through your descendants *because you obeyed My voice."*[26] This last phrase is expressed in the Torah as *"ekev asher shamata b'koli."*

Thus we can say the reason for Hashem's blessing was that Avraham listened to God's voice even when he was in a condition of *"ekev,"* in a condition of darkness and confusion like that of the souls of *ikvesa d'Meshicha.* The greatness of Avraham at the *akeidah* lay in his continuing to obey and believe even when he was like a "heel," when his mind was too weak to understand and his heart was too heavy to feel. Even when all the reasons for belief had disappeared and all the pillars of faith had fallen, Avraham continued to have faith — by faith alone.

---

22. Rav Mordechai of Lechovitch was a disciple of Rav Shlomo of Karlin. He is regarded today as the founder of Slonimer Chassidus.
23. *Devarim* 7:12.
24. See *Bereshis Rabbah* 42:3.
25. *Divrei Shalom* (Vilna: 1882), p. 60d.
26. *Bereshis* 22:16–18.

A SIGN FOR OUR TIMES

Just as Avraham succeeded in the test of the *akeidah*, just as he continued to serve God faithfully despite the darkness and confusion, so will it be with us, in the period prior to Mashiach, for the *akeidah* is a sign of what will happen in our own time.

The souls of our generation are well equipped for the trials of *ikvesa d'Meshicha*. Although a heel is numb, it is also extremely tough. Indeed, it is precisely the hardness and coarseness of the heel that enables it to bear the weight of the body and to survive even while it is being scraped and pounded against the ground.

In a very real sense, the entire body depends on the heel, for it is the heel which supports the body and carries it to its destination. Similarly, all the generations of Jewish history depend upon the final generation of *ikvesa d'Meshicha*, and the success of that generation will bring the endeavors of all the earlier generations to their ultimate realization. It is our generation, in overcoming the *nisyonos* of *ikvesa d'Meshicha*, which will carry the Jewish people from exile to redemption.

According to the book of *Daniel*, evildoers will abound during this period, but at the same time "the wise will understand."[27] They will understand that it is a test of faith, and they will remain strong in their *emunah*.

In that final and most difficult test, there will be Jews who are righteous and faithful. In the midst of darkness, they will continue to walk by the light of faith. Surrounded by confusion, they will be calm. In a world of uncertainty and doubt, they will remain faithful to Hashem, and their Heavenly glory will not be taken from them. They will live by a faith that is clear and luminous, as it is written in the book of *Daniel*: "The wise will shine with the splendor of the firmament, and those

---

27. *Daniel* 12:10.

who lead the multitude to righteousness will shine like the stars, forever and ever."[28]

We find a similar description in the message that was granted to the Jewish people just before the power of prophecy was taken away. There the prophet Malachi is also speaking about the period of *ikvesa d'Meshicha*. His message, like a special-delivery letter traversing the millennia, is addressed to a generation that is about to end its two-thousand-year voyage on the ocean of exile, a generation preparing to disembark on the shores of redemption. His words, telling of the arrival of Eliyahu Ha-Navi and the restoration of prophecy, are like a bridge connecting the earlier period of prophecy with the later one.

In that final prophecy, Malachi's words to the generation of *ikvesa d'Meshicha* are filled with both warning and encouragement. He describes a world in which wickedness is widespread, but he also promises that those who fear God will be protected: "A sun of righteousness will shine for those of you who fear My Name."[29]

In the merit of those who hold fast to *emunah* in the generation of *ikvesa d'Meshicha*, Israel will be redeemed. As *Chazal* tell us, "It is only in the merit of faith that the exiles will be redeemed."[30] And with the arrival of the redemption, all darkness and doubt will vanish like smoke, every question will receive a satisfying answer, and "the earth will be filled with the knowledge of God, as the waters fill the ocean."[31]

28. Ibid. 3.
29. *Malachi* 3:20.
30. *Midrash Tanchuma, Beshalach* 10; *Yalkut Shimoni, Beshalach* 240.
31. *Yeshayahu* 11:9. See *Mishneh Torah, Hilchos Melachim* 12:5.

3.
THE HIDDEN RESERVOIR OF FAITH
MORIAH AND MACHPEILAH

In the precious land that God gave to our fathers as a gift and inheritance, two places have always been especially cherished: Mount Moriah in Jerusalem and the cave of Machpeilah in Chevron. These are the places our Patriarchs purchased from the early inhabitants of the land at a price the Torah reckons in *"kesef malei,"* full silver.[1] In *lashon ha-kodesh* the word *kesef,* "silver," is related to the word *lichsof,* "to yearn." Thus the phrase *kesef malei* suggests the ecstatic yearnings and boundless love the Avos invested in the acquisition of these properties.

To appreciate the extraordinary qualities of these places — and their implications for us — we will need to look carefully at the words of the Torah and the commentaries of our Sages. As we proceed, we will begin to understand the difference between Moriah and Machpeilah, as well as the deep and hidden connection that unites them. Amid the questions and the answers, we may be able to glimpse, with God's help, a few rays of light from the glory of our *Beis Ha-Mikdash,* which was situated on Mount Moriah, and the splendor of

---

1. *Bereshis* 23:9; *Divrei Ha-Yamim* I 21:22, 24.

the chosen burial place of our forefathers in Chevron.

YERUSHALAYIM AND CHEVRON:
TWO PLACES OF PRAYER

When we study the *parashios* of *Sefer Bereshis* together with Rashi's commentary, we learn that Me'aras Ha-Machpeilah, the Machpeilah Cave in Chevron, is the resting place of our three Patriarchs and their wives: Avraham and Sarah, Yitzchak and Rivkah, Yaakov and Leah. In addition, Rashi informs us that the world's first couple, Adam Ha-Rishon and Chavah, are buried there also.[2] To understand the deeper significance of the Me'aras Ha-Machpeilah, however, we must turn to the words of our Sages, in the Gemara, the Midrash, and the mystical literature.

Chazal describe the greatness of the Me'aras Ha-Machpeilah in truly extraordinary terms. They tell us, for example, that it is the location of the entrance to Gan Eden, the doorway through which all souls must pass on their journey to the next world.[3]

Me'aras Ha-Machpeilah also has a special connection to prayer. According to the Gemara,[4] the *Avos* continue to pray there for the salvation of Israel even today, and the power of their prayers is such that if all three of them were allowed to pray simultaneously Mashiach would arrive at once.

It is not only the prayers of the *Avos* which are heard in the Machpeilah Cave. The prayers of every Jew pass through Me'aras Ha-Machpeilah as well.[5] In other words, it is a gateway through which our prayers can leave this world and enter the higher, Heavenly worlds. In modern terms, we might pic-

---

2. *Bereshis* 23:2; *Rashi*, s.v. *"b'Kiryas Arba."*
3. *Zohar* I:57b; *Zohar Chadash, Rus* 79d.
4. *Bava Metzia* 85b.
5. *Megaleh Amukos.*

ture it as a kind of communications tower that receives our whispered words of prayer and beams them upward to worlds we have never seen and cannot imagine.

Thus, according to *Chazal*, Me'aras Ha-Machpeilah plays a central role in the spiritual operation of the universe.

However it is very clear, from the Torah and from the words of our Sages, that Mount Moriah in Yerushalayim is also the gateway for our prayers. When Yaakov awoke from his dream on Mount Moriah, he exclaimed, *"Zeh sha'ar ha-Shamayim* — This is the gate of Heaven!"[6] And Rashi explains he was referring to this property of Mount Moriah — it is the place from which the prayers of Israel ascend to Heaven.

We also know from *Chazal* that Yerushalayim is a place which establishes a connection between Heaven and earth, between the spiritual world and the physical world. Yerushalayim has the power to connect Heaven and earth, because it is a city that exists as both an earthly place and a Heavenly presence — as *Yerushalayim shel Matah* and *Yerushalayim shel Malah.*[7] Yerushalayim is a double city, but not a divided city, for it is "the city joined together in unity."[8] In every stone of this luminous city, Heaven and earth coexist; and because Yerushalayim unites the worlds within itself, it also can connect the upper and lower worlds. Yerushalayim provides a link to Heaven for all of earth and a gateway for the prayers of *klal Yisrael.*

But if Yerushalayim provides a connection between Heaven and earth, why should there be another place, in Chevron, with the same properties? Doesn't it seem unnecessary?

---

6. *Bereshis* 28:17.
7. *Ta'anis* 5a; *Midrash Tehillim* 122:4.
8. *Tehillim* 122:3.

Another question, based on halachah: When we pray, we turn to face Yerushalayim. We direct our prayers toward Yerushalayim — not to Chevron. But if Machpeilah is the gateway for our prayers, shouldn't we face Chevron? Or, if both Yerushalayim and Chevron are gateways for our prayers, shouldn't we at least have the option of facing Chevron? But Jewish law clearly tells us to face Yerushalayim; it makes no mention of Chevron.

To answer these questions, we need to understand the differences between Chevron and Yerushalayim. Our first step, however, must be to recognize their similarities and the deep connection between them.

One Name and One Essence

According to the *Zohar*,[9] the very name Machpeilah reveals a connection between Chevron and Yerushalayim. The word *machpeilah* means a "double" or a "copy," and the *Zohar* suggests that Me'aras Ha-Machpeilah was called by this name because it is, in fact, a copy, a duplicate of Yerushalayim. Thus, every time we speak of Machpeilah we are emphasizing its similarity to Yerushalayim.

A name, especially a name given by the Torah, reveals the essence of the thing to which it refers. If the name Machpeilah means "duplicate of Yerushalayim," it must be that Chevron and Yerushalayim have, to a degree, the same spiritual essence. They deserve, in other words, to be regarded as two parts of the same larger entity. Thus, Me'aras Ha-Machpeilah is really an extension of Yerushalayim. True, it is territorially disconnected, separated by dozens of miles and buried beneath the stony soil of Chevron. But in essence, it belongs to the city of Yerushalayim. Thus, on the deepest level, Chevron

---

9. *Zohar* I:128b.

and Yerushalayim are one and the same, and that is why they both function as a gateway for our prayers.

The Holiness of the Avos

We can also appreciate that these two holy places, Chevron and Yerushalayim, share the same essence when we realize that they both draw their holiness from the same source: the forefathers of the Jewish people. In the case of Chevron, this is obvious. Not only was Chevron acquired for the Jewish people by Avraham Avinu, but it is also the place where the *Avos* continue to maintain a presence in the physical world. That is the uniqueness of Chevron, and that is the essence of its holiness.

While less obvious, it is no less true that the holiness of Yerushalayim is also an expression of the holiness of the *Avos*. For one thing, it was Avraham Avinu who established Yerushalayim as a place of prayer when, after the *akeidah*, he asked Hashem to make Mount Moriah a place of prayer for all the generations. We learn this from the verse ויקרא אברהם שם המקום ההוא ה' יראה אשר יאמר היום בהר ה' יראה.[10] Literally, the verse means "Avraham called that place by the name 'God Will See,' as it is said even today, 'God will appear on the mountain.'" According to the *Targum Onkelos*, however, it means, "Avraham served God and prayed in that place, and he said to God, 'May this be the place where the future generations will worship.' And therefore it is said, even today, 'This is the mountain where Avraham worshiped God.'"

Thus we see that it was Avraham who first designated Mount Moriah as a permanent place of prayer, winning it for the Jewish people by the strength of his prayers and the merit of his Divine service. In addition, *Targum Onkelos* tells us that it will be known forever as "the mountain where Avraham wor-

---

10. *Bereshis* 22:14.

shiped God." Now, if that is a name people use and a name recorded in the Torah, it must describe the essence of the place.
In other words, Mount Moriah is a place which openly expresses the holiness of Avraham Avinu, to the extent that every citizen of the world who refers to it will remember: "that is
the mountain where Avraham worshiped God."

There is yet another way we can recognize that the holiness of Yerushalayim is a reflection of the holiness of the *Avos*.
During the centuries when the *Beis Ha-Mikdash* stood, all of Israel would make the pilgrimage there three times a year, on
Pesach, Shavuos, and Sukkos.[11] In accordance with the
mitzvah known as *aliyah l'regel*, they would come "to see and to
be seen"[12] — to receive a revelation of Godliness and to stand
before Hashem. Each of these three festivals draws its holiness
from one of the three *Avos*, and that is the holiness which is revealed to the Jewish people at the time of each festival.[13] Thus,
the spiritual illumination *klal Yisrael* received in Yerushalayim
during the festivals was also an expression of the holiness of
the *Avos*, and through the mitzvah of *aliyah l'regel*,
Yerushalayim channeled that holiness to all of *klal Yisrael*.

Thus, we see that Chevron and Yerushalayim play the
same role in the process of prayer, they have the same name,
and they draw their holiness from the same source. Seeing that
in so many fundamental aspects they are identical, we are led
to the conclusion that, in essence, they are one. But how can
that be? One is a shining city on a hill, a beacon to the world,
while the other is a burial chamber, hidden beneath the surface
of the earth. How can a single essence be expressed in two such
antithetical ways?

---

11. *Shemos* 34:23–24.
12. See *Chagigah* 2a.
13. *Zohar* III:257b.

We can begin to solve this puzzle by looking more closely at the individual characteristics of these extraordinary places.

YERUSHALAYIM: CITY OF REVELATION, VISION, AND LIFE

Yerushalayim is a city of revelation. More than any other place in the world, it is the place that reveals Godliness and the connection between God and the Jewish people.

Yerushalayim is the place where God chose to build His House, the *Beis Ha-Mikdash*, in order to dwell among the Jewish people. The *Beis Ha-Mikdash* was an expression of God's love for us, and our Divine service in the *Beis Ha-Mikdash* — our work in elevating the material world to make it holy — was a living expression of our love for God. The *Beis Ha-Mikdash* was also known as the *Ohel Mo'ed* — the place appointed for God and His people to meet. As we said, it was the place to which all Israel came to "see and to be seen," to encounter the Divine and to receive a revelation of Godliness.

When we talk about a revelation of Godliness, it is Mount Sinai that usually comes to mind. However, Mount Sinai was a place of revelation for only a short time. It was the *Beis Ha-Mikdash* in Yerushalayim that was meant to provide a permanent home for the revelation of Sinai and to make that revelation continually accessible to the Jewish people. Thus, Yerushalayim is the place where Hashem chose to reveal His Presence to us — to make His Glory visible to us through the revelation of His Shechinah, the Divine Presence, and the light of His Countenance. That is why Yerushalayim is called *"Be-Har Hashem Yeira'eh* — "In the Mountain God Will Appear"[14] — for it is the place where God reveals Himself to His people, Israel.

---

14. *Bereshis* 22:14.

The revelation of Godliness in Yerushalayim during the time of the *Beis Ha-Mikdash* was so intense that even the physical world was visibly transformed. As we know from *Pirkei Avos*,[15] ten miracles took place continually in Yerushalayim. In the *Beis Ha-Mikdash*, for example, the thin column of smoke rising straight up from the altar was unaffected by even the strongest winds. Throughout the city as well, the miraculous coexisted comfortably with the commonplace. For centuries, no one was ever bitten by a snake in Yerushalayim, and even when the streets were filled with throngs of pilgrims, no one ever found himself without a night's lodging. It was a place where one could see the laws of the natural world bending, as if in a public display of deference to the laws of the spiritual world. In Yerushalayim, the heavy cloak with which the natural world usually conceals its Creator was thin to the point of transparency — no more than a diaphanous glove on the Hand of God.

Yerushalayim is revelation, and revelation is vision. Hence Yerushalayim is a mountain, for a mountain is visible from afar, and a mountain also grants the power of vision to those who stand upon it. Many of us have had the experience of traveling on a winding mountain road when suddenly a break in the trees reveals a breathtaking vista, and the landscape of a lovely green valley is spread out before our eyes — a meandering river, cultivated fields, a tiny herd of cows, and a toy-like village of little, white houses, all looking too delicate to be real. Perhaps it is the sudden expansion in the scope of one's vision or the novel experience of being able to examine an entire village like a page in a book, but such a view brings a kind of exhilaration even to the dullest heart and a moment of inspiration even to the coarsest mind.

---

15. *Avos* 5:5.

Yerushalayim is a mountain not only in the topographical sense, but also in the spiritual sense, and the breathtaking vistas that can be seen from its high places are spiritual landscapes. Those who prepared themselves with purity and devotion and found favor with God were able to ascend the "mountain of Hashem." From the heights of Yerushalayim, they saw visions of Godliness and heard the words of the Living God. With such a power of vision come inspiration, exhilaration, and exultation, and hence Yerushalayim is "a place of beautiful scenery, the joy of all the earth."[16]

Yerushalayim, where the Divine source of life was openly revealed, was a city characterized by an abundance of life and by the lively service of God. This activity and animation were evident, even at the dawn of Jewish history, in the Divine service of the *Avos* in Yerushalayim. Can we even imagine the effort and intensity with which the *Avos* gave themselves to God in prayer, or the magnitude of the Divine energy they drew down upon themselves, or the torrent of Godly light and vitality which came cascading into the world as they stood silently in prayer?

Later in history, the *Beis Ha-Mikdash* was a small city unto itself, brimming and bustling with the lively service of God. Speedy and diligent *kohanim* performed the Divine Temple service with pure thoughts and precise hands, and the air was filled with the sweet singing of the *Leviyim*. At times their music was soulful and beseeching like the yearning heart of a sincere penitent, and at times it was joyful and resonant, full of the humble gratitude of a soul that has found forgiveness and has come back to the arms of its loving Father in Heaven. This small city of God, this earthly palace of the Heavenly King, was surrounded at all hours of the day and night by an honor

---

16. *Tehillim* 48:3.

guard of vigilant servants, each sentry at his assigned post and each watch at its appointed time — an earthly echo of the orders of angels who surround the Heavenly Throne of Glory. It was a city where the animated service of God never ceased, like the ever-present fire on the altar — like the Godly Jewish soul itself, which is always striving upward in its desire to unite with God.

Thus, Yerushalayim has always been a place of spiritual illumination. And it is destined to be — may the day come very soon — the place of the great revelation at the culmination of history which will fill the earth "with the knowledge of God, as the waters fill the ocean."[17]

CHEVRON: THE HIDDEN PRESENCE OF THE AVOS

When we look at Chevron, we realize at once that it is the very opposite of revelation. In Chevron, the *Avos* are deeply hidden in a cave within a cave, far removed from sight. In contrast, Yerushalayim is a mountain which can be seen from afar. There, the *Avos* served God with animation and vitality, and Yaakov described it as "the place where my fathers prayed."[18] In Me'aras Ha-Machpeilah, however, the *Avos* are in a state of repose, a state Yaakov referred to with the words "I will lie down with my fathers."[19]

Previously we showed that Moriah and Machpeilah are, in essence, one. Now we see that this essence manifests itself in two diametrically opposite ways: Yerushalayim is revelation, and Chevron is concealment. Thus, we are led to the puzzling conclusion that Chevron is a kind of "underground Yerushalayim." The Me'aras Ha-Machpeilah seems to be con-

---

17. *Yeshayahu* 11:9.
18. *Bereshis* 28:17; *Rashi* s.v. *"ki im beis Elokim."*
19. *Bereshis* 47:30.

nected to Yerushalayim like an invisible sister-city, a distant, subterranean annex hidden beneath the rocks of Chevron. To understand the meaning of this, we must understand the way in which we ourselves are connected to the *Avos* — and to Chevron.

Our Connection to the Avos

We are the descendants of the *Avos.* But we are not merely the end product of a long process of development of which they were the beginning. If that were the extent of our connection to the *Avos*, we would only be their distant relatives, and we would possess within ourselves no more than a pale glimmer of what they were. In fact, our connection to the *Avos* is far more intimate and essential. The *Avos* are at the very center of our identity; they are an integral part of our being.

The mystical tradition tells us that we, together with all the Jewish souls of all the generations, are included, in a spiritual sense, *within* the *Avos*. This is a profound idea that is not easy to understand. One way to approach it is to remember that *Chazal* often use the word *av* to refer to a general category that includes a number of items which are called its *tolados* — the "offspring" or "offshoots" of the *av*. In the laws of Shabbos, for example, there are thirty-nine *avos melachos*, primary categories of forbidden labors.[20] *Tochein*, grinding or milling grain is one such category. Two of its *tolados* are chopping vegetables into very small pieces and grinding a solid piece of metal into a powder. In a similar way, since our Patriarchs are given the name *Avos*, this is a hint that they are like a general category that *includes* its *tolados*.

Another way to approach this idea is with the analogy of a seed. A single acorn can grow into a towering oak with dozens

---

20. *Shabbos* 7:2.

of branches and thousands of leaves. And yet, in some sense, the tiny seed already contains within itself the entire tree and even the later generations of trees that will be derived from the seed.

Similarly, there was a time when the *Avos* were the only Jews in the world, and hence we can say that all the future generations of Israel were contained within them. The souls which would later be born into the world in a revealed and physical way already had a hidden, spiritual existence within the *Avos* themselves. Thus, at that earliest stage of Jewish history, we lived within the *Avos*, so to speak, and each of our souls, according to its nature, formed a particular part of the *Avos*.[21]

Today, however, the situation is in a sense reversed. Each of our souls retains its original identity as a part of the *Avos*, and hence the *Avos* continue to exist within us.[22] But more than this, it is not only a *particular* aspect of the *Avos* that is present today within each individual Jewish soul — it is the very *essence* of the *Avos*, their essential being.

A Me'aras Ha-Machpeilah within Every Heart

This idea that each Jewish soul contains the essence of the *Avos* is also not easy to understand. But it is related to the mystical concept that every individual is a microcosm — a small world that contains, in miniature, everything found in the world at large.[23]

Since each individual is a microcosm, and since in the world at large there is a place we call Me'aras Ha-Machpeilah, which contains the *Avos*, it follows that each individual must possess within himself his own private Me'aras Ha-

---

21. *Tikkunei Zohar, tikkun* 69, p. 109b.
22. This is, of course, in addition to the continued existence of the souls of the *Avos* in Gan Eden.
23. *Tikkunei Zohar* 130b.

Machpeilah. It is a place deep within his heart that contains the essential being of the *Avos* and their holiness. Although it is so deeply hidden that even the individual himself cannot directly sense its presence, it is there nonetheless.

This means that whenever a Jew prays, it is as if he is praying together with the *Avos* — and this greatly helps his prayer. This is because it was the *Avos* who established the practice of regular prayer, fixing it firmly and forever in the soul of Israel.[24] It was they, through their unceasing service and absolute devotion, who opened the gates and pathways of prayer for themselves and for all their descendants. The *Avos* forged a connection between themselves and God, and that same connection is automatically available to us. Their connection to God was so deep that it became an essential part of their being, and their essential being is within us.

As a result, a Jew who wishes to approach God in prayer need not clear a new path for himself. Since he is a part of the *Avos*, and since their essence is within him, he can follow in their footsteps and use the same pathways that they established for all the generations.

The Berachah of Avos: Finding a Connection

That is why our most important daily prayer, the *Shemoneh Esreh,* begins with the blessing called *Avos.* The *Shemoneh Esreh* is the prayer in which, after we have prepared ourselves by reciting *Pesukei d'Zimrah* and the blessings of *Shema,* we attempt to attach ourselves most closely to God. Standing still and silent, we try to quiet the constant chatter of self-awareness and to feel as near to God as a silently spoken word is near to the one who speaks it.

But how can we accomplish this? Do we harbor any point

---

24. *Berachos* 26b.

of spirituality uncluttered with self-awareness? Do we have any place within us that can serve as an initial point of connection with the Divine? And which aspect of God should we attempt to know and relate to first?

In answer to these questions, the first blessing of *Shemoneh Esreh* tells us that when we first approach God we should address Him as *"Elokei Avraham, Elokei Yitzchak, v'Elokei Yaakov."* We are reminded that deep within us, hidden below the level of self-awareness, there is a Me'aras Ha-Machpeilah, where the essence of the *Avos* is our essence and the connection between the *Avos* and God is our connection. It is as if the first blessing of the *Shemoneh Esreh* is telling us, "Do you want to find God? He is *Elokei Avraham* — He can be located and identified by His attachment to the *Avos*, and the essence of the *Avos* is within you."

Thus, the first blessing of the *Shemoneh Esreh* invites a Jew to connect himself to the *Avos*, so that his prayer may ascend together with their prayers. And where can he find the *Avos*? Within the Me'aras Ha-Machpeilah of his own heart, at the very core of his being. This is the spiritual meaning of the idea that the prayers of Israel ascend to Heaven by way of the Me'aras Ha-Machpeilah.

A Place Removed from the World of Place

We have come to understand that there is a spiritual Me'aras Ha-Machpeilah deep within the heart of every Jew, and it corresponds to the physical Me'aras Ha-Machpeilah in the world at large. As one would expect, the spiritual realities of the inner Machpeilah are closely mirrored by the physical details of its worldly counterpart.

The spiritual Machpeilah within our hearts is so close to the center of our being that it is not generally accessible to our awareness. It is so deeply hidden that it cannot be directly perceived. And, of course, being a spiritual entity, it does not take up any space, and it cannot be assigned to any particular location.

In the physical world, to be sure, there is a place in Chevron where the Me'aras Ha-Machpeilah is located. Because of the constraints of the natural world, there must be a particular place on earth where the *Avos* are buried. But when we look carefully at the details of the burial site in Chevron, we see that although it is located in the material world, it is almost entirely removed from the limitations that a physical existence usually imposes.

When one stands on the ground in Chevron, one cannot see a grave or tomb, although one knows there is a cave beneath the ground. And even if one were to catch a glimpse of the entrance of the cave, that is not the place where the *Avos* are buried, for, as the name Machpeilah indicates, the *Avos* are buried in a cave within a cave or, according to another opinion, in a cave beneath a cave.[25]

They are not buried in a single cave because that would not be a complete concealment. If someone were to stand at the entrance of the cave, he could peer within. Therefore the cave that conceals the *Avos* is itself concealed by a second cave, and from the ground above, both caves are invisible.

Thus, in the physical world, the *Avos* are so deeply hidden that we cannot locate them. They are present, but not in a way that is expressed within the usual parameters of space and location. They are present, and yet they are removed from the world of place.

Similarly, in the spiritual world, in the Machpeilah that exists within the heart of every Jew, the essence of the *Avos* is so deeply hidden that it is practically undetectable. It is hidden

---

25. *Eiruvin* 83a.

far beneath the thoughts and feelings that flicker across the face of our being, shifting like the winds and changing like the weather. It is hidden beneath the persistent patterns of personality; it is deeper than the difference between wise and foolish, deeper even than the good and evil we do — the essence of the *Avos* is at the very center of our being.

CHEVRON: THE INDESTRUCTIBLE CONNECTION

Why, we might ask, in both the physical Machpeilah in Chevron and the spiritual Machpeilah within our hearts, is the holiness so deeply hidden? This concealment might seem a purely negative characteristic, an indication of Chevron's inferiority to Yerushalayim. However, it is precisely this characteristic that is the key to the unique excellence of Chevron, to the aspect in which it surpasses Yerushalayim.

The reason why the holiness of the *Avos* in Chevron is so deeply hidden is related — by way of a distant metaphor — to the reason why treasure chests were once buried beneath the beaches of desolate, inaccessible islands and why governments today consign gold bullion to underground vaults with thick steel doors. It is to protect that which is precious and irreplaceable.

Let us recall that the city of Yerushalayim was destroyed as a result of our sins, and the *Beis Ha-Mikdash*, once teeming with the vibrant service of God, was left desolate and solitary. The glory of Yerushalayim was taken from it, and in the place where all of Israel had come "to see and to be seen," the open revelation of the Divine Presence was interrupted.

The revelation of the holiness of the *Avos* was also removed from Yerushalayim. Today we can no longer go up to worship in the *Beis Ha-Mikdash* three times a year. Hence, the holiness of these festivals, which is drawn from the holiness of the *Avos*, is no longer available to us in full measure. When the *Beis*

Ha-Mikdash was destroyed, the spiritual presence of the *Avos*, which was the essence of the *Beis Ha-Mikdash*, was also taken from Yerushalayim.

But Me'aras Ha-Machpeilah was never destroyed; it was never even affected by the *churban*, the destruction of the *Beis Ha-Mikdash*. Indeed, if we look deeply at Chevron, we realize that it is a place which, by its very nature, could never be subject to *churban*. *Churban*, in the spiritual sense, consists of several elements. One is *hester panim*, the concealment of God's involvement with us. Another is *histalkus ha-Shechinah*, the removal of the open revelation of the Divine Presence, and the third is the cessation of the service of God as performed by man.

In Yerushalayim, God's involvement with His people was open and manifest, a situation known as *he'aras panim*. In addition, the Divine Presence was revealed, and the Jewish people were energetically devoted to the active service of God. Since it was possible for these to be suspended — for the revealed can be hidden, and human activity can be halted — it was also possible for there to be a *churban* in Yerushalayim.

The Machpeilah, on the other hand, was never a place of open revelation. The *Avos* are concealed there in secrecy. Nor was it ever a place characterized by the active service of God, for the *Avos* came to the Machpeilah only after they had concluded their days of active service upon the earth. It is a place, therefore, which is not susceptible to the forces of *churban*. Anything that *churban* has the power to destroy was never to be found in Chevron. As a result, that which does exist in Chevron — the deeply hidden holiness of the *Avos* — is completely invulnerable to *churban*.

This is a reflection of an important general idea: only those aspects of holiness which are in a state of revelation are susceptible to *churban*. There are deeper levels of holiness, however, that are always in a state of concealment, and they can never be affected by *churban*. In the language of our mystical tradition: "In the aspect that is concealed [*beVechinas Iskassiyah*], there is no *churban*."[26]

Churban is a phenomenon of this world. It affects only the physical world, or those aspects of spirituality that are openly revealed in the physical world. To put it in even simpler terms, *churban* affects the spiritual world only insofar as it *appears* to us, but not as it actually *is*. Spiritual realities as they are in essence — on a level deeper than revelation — are untouched by *churban*.

Thus, there is an aspect of the Divine Presence and the holiness of the *Avos* which is deeper than revelation. And that essence of their holiness continues to be present within us, even in our state of exile, although it is present, to be sure, only in a concealed way.

The Secret of the Exile

This is the spiritual reality to which Me'aras Ha-Machpeilah alludes, and, in fact, it is the *sod ha-galus* — the very "secret of the exile." It is the key to what *galus* is, and it is the secret hidden by the *galus* itself. The secret of the exile is that, within the multiple concealments and the thick darkness of the *galus*, there resides a holiness — a holiness of an even higher level than the holiness that can be expressed in open revelation. In *galus*, the light of Godliness is clothed and covered and again concealed, until it appears to our eyes as nothing more than darkness. But within that darkness, the holiness is present. *Galus* only has the power to *conceal* Godliness, not to *remove* it from us. Within the very circumstances we experience as a concealment, God is present.

---

26. See *Pelach Ha-Rimon, Shemos*, p. 7, quoting the *Ba'al Ha-Tanya*.

This has been true of the *galus* from the moment it began. *Chazal* tell us that at the very instant of the *churban*, even as Hashem was removing His Presence, on a revealed level, from Yerushalayim, He was also taking an oath that His Presence, on a hidden level, would never depart from the Jewish people. And so, when the exiles went out from Yerushalayim, the Shechinah went with them, as our Sages comment on the verse "All the glory of Zion has gone out."[27]

Nevuchadnetzar and Titus could order their armies into Yerushalayim to destroy the *Beis Ha-Mikdash*, but they were powerless to reach the gates which guard the holy center of the Jewish soul. At that still and timeless center where the Jewish soul is connected to God, the *churban*, with all its sound and fury, could not inflict even the slightest damage. The tyrants of the world have a power to affect only the external aspects of our connection to God. This is what the verse in *Megillas Esther* is hinting at when it states, "Haman came into the *outer* court-yard of the king's palace."[28] But all the wicked tyrants cannot make even the slightest change in the innermost aspects of our souls. On these deepest levels, we are connected to God in a way that is invulnerable to *churban* and can never be inter-rupted.

Chevron: Chibbur in the Midst of Churban

This, then, is the spiritual meaning of Me'aras Ha-Machpeilah. In a time of *churban* — when the revelation of holiness has ceased from its place — the Machpeilah, which is enduring, in-visible, and invulnerable, shows us that the essence of the holi-ness within us is also enduring, invisible, and invulnerable.

Stones turn to dust, monuments crumble, and the ideolo-

---

27. *Eichah* 1:6.
28. *Esther* 6:4.

gies that men devise are rejected and abandoned, but the holiness within us is timeless. Fire and ruin may scar the face of the earth, but the holiness within us is intact. And if there comes a time when the streets are awash in the waters of impurity and the air itself is polluted with uncleanness, even then the holiness within us will be pure and pristine.

Thus, Chevron declares that even when the Divine Presence is no longer openly revealed to us, we are deeply and inseparably connected to our Father in Heaven. Indeed, the very name Chevron expresses this. The Hebrew word *chevron* (חברון) is spelled with exactly the same letters as the word *churban* (חורבן), but the letters have been rearranged to suggest the word *chibbur* (חיבור), which means "connection" or "attachment." In other words, the name Chevron tells us that even in the midst of *churban* we are still in a state of *chibbur* — connected to our Father in Heaven.

True, this connection is not openly visible, and the wicked tyrants, boasting that they have banished the nation and its God, gleefully imagine that they have driven God away from His people, Israel. But there will come a time when God's Kingship will once again be revealed, and all the world will recognize the error of the tyrants — for the truth is that we were always connected to God.

A Concealment within a Concealment

In *parashas Vayeilech*, we find a warning about a period in history when the Divine Presence will be completely hidden from us. There may come a time, Hashem tells Moshe, when "I will utterly hide [*haster astir*] My Face."[29] The use of the double form of the Hebrew verb — *haster astir* — is understood by our Sages as an ominous warning of a *hester besoch hester*, a concealment

---

29. *Devarim* 31:18.

within a concealment.

What is this double degree of concealment? If men are afflicted by troubles, God forbid, yet they remain aware that God is responsible for everything and that it is He who is hiding Himself within everything, even within their troubles, then this is only a single degree of concealment. But when the very fact that it is God who is concealed by the events of the world is itself concealed, and people think to themselves, *It is because God is no longer with me that I have been afflicted by these troubles*,[30] then this is a double degree of concealment. It is a frighteningly complete concealment, because even the fact that it is a concealment has been concealed. May God protect us in such a time!

It is just such a double degree of concealment, such a *hester besoch hester*, to which Me'aras Ha-Machpeilah alludes, with its own double concealment, its cave within a cave. And the Machpeilah tells us that despite the doubled and redoubled darkness of the *galus* God is indeed in our midst, and our connection to God on the deepest level can never be broken.

CHEVRON — GUARDIAN OF ETERNITY

Now that we have come to appreciate the spiritual meaning of Chevron, we can better understand its relationship to Yerushalayim.

The *Beis Ha-Mikdash* in Yerushalayim was a "House of prayer for all the nations."[31] It provided the world with a gateway for prayer, and so, when Yerushalayim was destroyed, one might have thought that the gateway for our prayers was also lost. But the Machpeilah tells us otherwise. Even when the *Beis Ha-Mikdash* is destroyed, the Machpeilah proclaims that

---

30. Ibid., 17.
31. *Yeshayahu* 56:7.

the essence of the *Avos* is intact within us, and the pathways of prayer that they prepared are still available to us. Thus, on the deepest level, the connection provided by Yerushalayim is permanent, because Chevron and Yerushalayim share a common essence, and Chevron is indestructible.

There is another sense in which Chevron teaches us the permanence of Yerushalayim. Once we learn the lesson of Chevron — that the hidden aspects of holiness are invulnerable to *churban* and continue to be present in a hidden way — we can apply this to the original Machpeilah, to Yerushalayim itself. In this way, Chevron teaches us that in Yerushalayim, even in its state of destruction, the Divine Presence continues to be present in its beloved, protected place. Although it is hidden from our eyes, the Shechinah of our Almighty God is still hovering in peaceful majesty within the hidden, inner chambers of its holy palace.

This is what the Maggid of Koznitz means when he says that the destruction of the *Beis Ha-Mikdash* was only a matter of outward appearance.[32] *Churban* is an outward show, an all too vivid and convincing presentation which is, in truth, no more than an external facade. On the level of essential reality, the *Beis Ha-Mikdash* continues to exist in a state of consummate perfection.

Why Weren't the Avos Buried in Yerushalayim?

Although we know that Chevron is an extension of Yerushalayim, we might feel that the *Avos* should have been buried in the original Yerushalayim, near Mount Moriah. Surely that would have been more appropriate, for Mount Moriah is the location in the physical world that corresponds most precisely to what the *Avos* are in the spiritual world.

---

32. *Yakar Me-Paz, Re'eh.*

Yerushalayim is the starting point of Creation, the first place in the world that was brought into existence by God's word. Under Mount Moriah lies the *even shesiyah*, the primordial stone which was formed at the very outset of Creation as a foundation for the world.[33] It is the place that preceded and gave rise to all the other places on the globe. It is, in a sense, the embryo of the earth.

In similar way, the *Avos* are the starting point and source of the Jewish people and the Jewish soul. They are our "founding fathers"; their lives provide the basis for our lives, both biologically and spiritually, and their actions established the architecture of the Jewish soul for all generations.

So, on the face of it, it would seem that the *Avos*, the world's first Jews, should have been buried in Yerushalayim, which is the world's first place. Why weren't they?

It is precisely because our connection to the *Avos* is deeper than anything that can be made manifest and visible — and deeper even than our connection to Yerushalayim — that the *Avos* could not be buried in Yerushalayim.

Yerushalayim is a place where sin had the power to bring *churban*; it is vulnerable to sin. The Machpeilah, on the other hand, is immune to *churban* and impervious to sin. Like the Machpeilah, our connection to the *Avos* is also unaffected by sin. The aspect of the *Avos* that lives within us is a spark that cannot be extinguished by all the waters of the world. It is so deep within us and so much a part of us that it cannot be defiled by any contact with impurity — like wine still hidden within the grapes.

In fact, this is what Yaakov Avinu was praying for when he said, "May my soul not enter their counsel."[34] In asking that his

---

33. *Bemidbar Rabbah* 12:4.
34. *Bereshis* 49:6. See *Rashi* s.v. "*Be-sodam.*"

name not be mentioned in connection with the sins of his children, he was really requesting, according to the Ohr Ha-Chayim,[35] that the harmful effect of any sins committed by his descendants should not be permitted to reach the holiness of Yaakov Avinu that is present within their souls.

If the *Avos* had been buried in Yerushalayim, which was susceptible to *churban*, this would have signified that the aspect of the *Avos* we have within us is also susceptible to destruction and nullification. Therefore they could only be buried outside Yerushalayim, in a place that would remain intact and inviolate even when Yerushalayim lay in ruins due to our sins. And there, in Chevron, they provide a sign for Israel that even in a period of *churban*, we are in a state of *chibbur* — connected to our Father in Heaven.

SEEING BENEATH THE SURFACE

For long stretches of history, Chevron has presented a face to the world that seems to be strangely lacking in holiness. Deep beneath the ground the *Avos* rest in hidden splendor, but above them, in broad daylight, the wicked walk with impunity. Their unclean structures cover the sacred ground like thorns and brambles surrounding a rose, and with brazen effrontery they lay claim to the holy site and attempt to appropriate it as their own.

It was in describing Chevron that the *meraglim*, the spies sent by Moshe, said, "And there we saw the titans, the sons of the giant, a descendant of the original titans."[36] On the surface, Chevron presented itself as an impenetrable stronghold of wicked giants, a city overrun by the progeny of fallen angels. But what the spies did not see — could not see — for it is not

---

35. *Ohr Ha-Chayim* on *Bereshis* 49:6, s.v. *"Achein."*
36. *Bemidbar* 13:33.

there in a state of open revelation, was the powerful holiness of the *Avos* concealed below.

At the beginning of *parashas Chayei Sarah*, the Torah refers to Chevron as Kiryas Arba, and Rashi offers two explanations for the name.[37] First, he informs us that Kiryas Arba was named after four giants who lived there: Achiman, Sheishai, Talmai, and their father. Then, as a second explanation, Rashi suggests that the name refers to the four couples buried there: Adam and Chavah, Avraham and Sarah, Yitzchak and Rivka, Yaakov and Leah.

Rashi's first explanation is in itself rather puzzling. Why would the Torah choose to refer to the holy site of Chevron with a name that commemorates four wicked giants who briefly darkened the place with their cursed presence? And why does Rashi offer this explanation first, as if to give it precedence? Indeed, why does Rashi even need both explanations?

But in the light of what we now know about Chevron, we see that both explanations are necessary to convey the true nature and significance of Chevron. An outward appearance of wickedness, a surface that does not reveal Godliness, and hidden deeply within, the original and essential holiness of the Jewish people — *that* is Chevron. The wickedness, like the giants, is transient, while the holiness, like the holiness of the *Avos*, endures — protected and pristine and in all its powerful glory — until the end of time.

A Portrait of a Jew

Rashi's characterization of Chevron can also be read as a description of an individual Jew, for, as we have said, every individual is a microcosm, with his own hidden Machpeilah. On this level, Rashi's words describe a Jew who has become en-

---

37. *Bereshis* 23:2; *Rashi*, s.v. *"b'Kiryas Arba."*

snared in sin and seems to be entirely overpowered by his own wickedness —"overrun by wicked giants," so to speak. When we look at him, we cannot see even the faintest glimmer of his original and essential Jewish holiness. But Chevron teaches us that the picture of utter destruction this Jew presents to the world is only a matter of outward appearance. Deep within him, hidden from our eyes, the full holiness of the *Avos* endures. If he will only make up his mind to return to God, that unblemished aspect of the *Avos* will provide him with a foundation on which to rebuild his house. If he will only return, that inviolable reservoir will once again fill him with a revealed and perceptible holiness.

Rashi mentions the giants first, not because what they represent is more true, but because that is the order in which we see the world. When we look at Chevron, or at another Jew, we notice the outward appearance first. Only later, after much reflection, do we become aware of the deeper reality — the holiness of the *Avos* that is hidden beneath the surface.

WHY WE DON'T FACE CHEVRON WHEN WE PRAY

Now we can also understand why we don't face Chevron when we pray, why instead we turn to face Yerushalayim. True, both Chevron and Yerushalayim are "Machpeilahs" — places with a double presence, with a Heavenly address as well as an earthly one. Both are places that join worlds and can serve as gateways for our prayers. But there is an important difference between them.

Yerushalayim, as we have shown, is the place most closely identified with God's revealed Presence in the world. It was to Yerushalayim that Jews traveled three times a year to experience the Divine Presence, "to see and to be seen."

Chevron, on the other hand, is the place which proclaims that our deepest connection to God does not depend on any particular place. Chevron teaches us that even when we have lost the place of the Divine Presence, the Divine Presence is still with us — and within us. In addition, Chevron is a place so deeply hidden from the world of visible appearance that it has ceased, in effect, to exist within that world — and hence its significance is also not dependent on its physical, geographical location.

Therefore, turning toward Chevron when we pray would not only be irrelevant; it would be inconsistent with the lesson Chevron teaches us. To point to Chevron is to miss the point that Chevron makes!

On the other hand, to point to Yerushalayim and to direct our prayers toward it, even in the geographical sense, *is* entirely fitting. The essential character of Yerushalayim is that it is a place that is known and noticeable — a distinguished place.

In fact, Yerushalayim is not only a distinguished place; of all the places in the world, it is the most distinguished place. Yerushalayim is so uniquely well-known that the Torah can refer to it simply as *ha-makom*, "the place." When Yaakov Avinu arrived at Mount Moriah for the first time, the Torah tells us, "*Va-yifga ba-makom* — He happened upon the place."[38] Although the Torah does not explicitly identify this place, Rashi informs us that *ha-makom* means Yerushalayim.[39]

Ordinarily, it is only meaningful to speak of "the place" if one has already specified a particular place. But Yerushalayim is different. It is unique. Yerushalayim is so much the focus of our thoughts and the center of our attention that the Torah can simply say "the place," and we know that it means Yerushalayim. Yerushalayim is intrinsically endowed with

---

38. *Bereshis* 28:11.
39. *Rashi* loc. cit., s.v. "*Va-yifga ba-makom.*"

distinction. It is permanently chosen.

There is an even deeper reason why the Torah refers to Yerushalayim as "the place." We know that Yerushalayim is the starting point of Creation, the place that preceded and gave rise to all the other places of the earth. In the dimension of space,[40] Yerushalayim is the *reishis*, the beginning.

Similarly, in the dimension of time, the *reishis* of the year is Rosh Ha-Shanah. Rosh Ha-Shanah is the starting point of time, the day from which all the other days of the year draw their existence. That is why the Torah can say "today," as it does in *parashas Nitzavim*,[41] and the real meaning is Rosh Ha-Shanah.[42] Every day of the calendar, every "today," is an extension of Rosh Ha-Shanah. [43]

Similarly, the Torah refers to Yerushalayim as "the place" because every other place is derived from and draws its existence from Yerushalayim. A place provides a "possibility of being" for all the objects that exist there. Yerushalayim, however, provides a "possibility of being" for all the places of the world, and so it deserves to be called "the place of all places," or simply "the place." Thus Yerushalayim is a distinguished place, a place which is by nature "pointed out" and visible. In addition, it is a place of revelation, and so we turn to face Yerushalayim when we pray in order to receive the revelation and the light

---

40. According to *Sefer Yetzirah* 3:3, the world was created in three dimensions: space, time, and soul.

41. *Devarim* 29:9.

42. *Zohar* II:32b, III:231a; see *Ramaz*.

43. It is interesting to note that the numerical value of the Hebrew words *rosh ha-shanah* is equal to that of *beis ha-mikdash*. This can be understood according to the idea, found in *Sefer Yetzirah*, that the dimensions of time and space are parallel. Since Rosh Ha-Shanah is the *reishis* in time and the *Beis Ha-Mikdash* is located at the *reishis* in space, they are in a sense equivalent, and this is reflected by their numerical values.

that Yerushalayim provides.

But our connection to God is deeper than revelation. Through Chevron and the Machpeilah that is hidden in the Jewish heart, we are connected to God in a way that cannot be revealed, but can also never be destroyed. Chevron tells us that even in a time of *churban* we are still attached to God, and we can pray together with the *Avos*. Thus it is Chevron which provides us with our deepest and most permanent potential for prayer.

When we pray, we pray with Chevron and by means of Chevron. But we do not turn to face Chevron — because we do not need to! Chevron is within us. It is not something external, like a source of light we must face in order to see. Chevron is the deepest level of our being; it is the essence of who we are. When we pray, we look *towards* Yerushalayim to receive a revelation of the Divine Presence, but we pray *from* Chevron, from the point within our being where we are permanently connected with the *Avos* and with our Creator.

MARRIAGE AND METAPHOR

Up to this point, we have discussed the spiritual significance of Yerushalayim and Chevron. By examining the characteristics of these places, we have come to understand that they provide us with two different connections to God: one revealed and one concealed.

In the rest of this chapter, we will use these ideas to gain a deeper understanding of the actions of the *Avos*. We can understand, for example, why the *Avos* considered it so important that both they and their wives should be buried in the Machpeilah, and also the significance of the fact that Yaakov did not bury Rachel in Chevron. Before considering these questions, however, we need to understand one key idea: the spiritual meaning of a Jewish marriage.

Every Jewish marriage is a metaphor, a tiny model of an immensely great and holy reality. A Jewish marriage is an echo of the Heavenly marriage by which the Jewish people are connected to God. In the writings of the Prophets, God is often described as a bridegroom and the Jewish people as His bride. The entire book of *Shir Ha-Shirim* is based on this metaphor.

One can speak about a Jewish marriage on two levels: revealed and concealed. The revealed level — the level of *Isgalia* — deals only with what is visible in the world, and so it deals only with the aspects of a marriage that are related to the body. On this level, a marriage is a relationship with social, emotional, and biological dimensions. It begins with the halachic act of *kiddushin* and lasts for as long as a couple are together in this world.

There is, however, a deeper, concealed level — the level of *Iskassia* — and it takes into consideration the aspects of a marriage that relate to the soul and are not directly visible. *Chazal* tell us that in every marriage the souls of the bridegroom and the bride were connected to one another long before the wedding. Years before their union was a even a glimmer of inspiration in a matchmaker's mind, the souls of the *chasan* and *kallah* were already linked in Heaven.[44]

The Gemara tells us that at the very moment of conception, forty days before an embryo is given the form of a human being, a Divine voice echoes through the Heavens and proclaims the following: *"Bas ploni l'ploni* — This particular girl is meant to be the bride of this particular boy."[45] Thus, even at the earliest moments of life, when a soul first enters the world of time, its future partner in marriage has already been designated and announced in Heaven.

---

44. *Zohar* I:85b; III:43b; *Vayikra Rabbah* 29:8.
45. *Sotah* 2a.

Kiddushin: Revealing the Invisible Connection

In this light, it is clear that the halachic act of *kiddushin*, the Jewish marriage ceremony, does not "create" a marriage from nothing. On a hidden, spiritual level, the *chasan* and *kallah* were always connected to one another. The effect of the act of *kiddushin* is simply to strengthen that connection and to make it manifest. It turns an invisible connection into a public fact, and it imposes a set of legal obligations and restrictions.

Rarely, however, do ordinary people think about a marriage in these terms. Hidden, spiritual connections do not affect the way they view the world, and hence most people talk about a marriage as if it were engineered by the decisions of a few individuals. But that is what the Midrash calls: "*kazav bnei ish* — the lies of ordinary men."[46] It is a way of speaking that reflects a distorted picture of reality. In truth, every *chasan* and *kallah* were "*heimah me-hevel yachad* — they were together from the time they were a *hevel*,"[47] an insubstantial wisp of spirit, an incipient speck of life.

David and Batsheva

It is written in the Book of Samuel[48] that King David was punished by Hashem because of his marriage to Batsheva. A superficial reading of the story would give the impression that David's marriage to Batsheva was a complete mistake and that David took a woman who was never intended for him. The Gemara,[49] however, tells us a story that is much deeper and more mysterious. David was *supposed* to marry Batsheva. From the time the world was created, Batsheva was meant to be King David's wife.

---

46. *Vayikra Rabbah* 29:8.
47. *Tehillim* 62:10.
48. *Shmuel* II, ch. 11, 12.
49. *Sanhedrin* 107a.

In addition, the Rambam[50] tells us that Mashiach will be a descendant of King Shlomo, who was the son of David and Batsheva. This means that Batsheva carried within herself the seed of Mashiach; when David married her, he was establishing the royal line that would eventually bring the Mashiach into the world. According to some commentators,[51] David himself knew this through *ruach ha-kodesh*, Divine inspiration. He understood that Batsheva was the woman who would one day give him an heir to the throne, and that was the reason why he was attracted to her.

But if this is true, that David was meant to marry her, why was he punished? What did he do wrong?

David's error, the Gemara[52] explains, had to do with how he made Batsheva his wife. Although his actions were legally permissible, they were tainted by an appearance of impropriety. Had David been more patient, had he waited for a more appropriate moment, Batsheva would have become his wife in some other fashion, and their marriage would have been beyond reproach. As it was, however, David acted too soon, and he took Batsheva in a way that the Gemara describes as *"machov"* — a way that brought pain and suffering and that was marred by a faint suggestion of sin.

In explaining this idea, the Gemara quotes a verse from the book of Psalms[53] in which David himself declares, כי אני לצלע נכון ומכאובי נגדי תמיד — which is usually translated: "I am accustomed to trouble, and my pain is always before me." According to this translation, however, it is hard to see the relevance of the verse. Where, for example, is there a hint in the words that

---

50. *Peirush Ha-Mishnayos, Sanhedrin, perek Chelek*, principle 12.
51. Rav Tzadok Ha-Kohen, *Takanas Ha-Shavim* (Kratka), p. 42b.
52. *Sanhedrin* 107a.
53. *Tehillim* 38:18.

Batsheva was meant to be David's wife from the time the world was created?

The Maharsha explains that the Gemara's intention hinges on the word *tzela*, which can also mean "rib." The Gemara understands it as an allusion to the rib from which God created a wife for Adam, the first man. Hence, by extension, the word *tzela* is understood to mean "wife." In other words, David is saying, "I chose the proper *tzela*, the proper wife; however, my mistake, the fact that I took her in a way that caused pain, is always before me, and I can never forget it."

A Source in Unity

Let us understand this more deeply. If only the first wife, Chavah, was actually created from her husband's rib, why should the word *tzela* refer to other wives? Here, for example, the Gemara understands it to mean David's wife.

The answer is that, on a very deep level, whatever occurred to Adam and Chavah also occurs to their descendants. This is because in a hidden, spiritual sense, Adam and Chavah contained within themselves all the souls of their descendants.[54]

Initially, Hashem created Adam and Chavah as a single, unified being. Within that being, the souls of every *chasan* and *kallah* who would later be derived from Adam and Chavah were also united. Later, Hashem split that being into two separate halves, one male and one female; and so it is, in a spiritual sense, with their descendants. Every *chasan* and *kallah* are also created as one. *Heimah me-hevel yachad* — from the time they were created, from the time they were no more than a breath of spirit, they were together.

The beginning of every couple is unity. Every *chasan* and

---

54. This idea was explained earlier in this chapter, in connection with the *Avos*, and it applies similarly to Adam and Chavah.

kallah originate as one, and from that primordial, timeless unity their souls are sundered. Then, as separate beings, they descend through the supernal worlds, level after level, until each soul can be clothed in a physical body. They are born separately, a baby boy and a baby girl, each in a particular time and place, with all the details of identity that accompany the life of an individual in this world. The two children grow up, living lives that are seemingly independent and unconnected, until the appointed day when, by one of the great and incomprehensible mysteries of Divine Providence, a meeting is arranged. That is the moment when he discovers the lost half of his being and she discovers hers. Then through the mitzvos of *chuppah* and *kiddushin*, the original unity of their souls is reaffirmed and revealed in this world.[55]

An Eternal Edifice

Since the hidden connection between the *chasan* and *kallah* is a spiritual connection, it is permanent. Since it is not a part of the material world, it is not affected by the vicissitudes of life. Since it is the result of a unity of souls and a shared spiritual identity, even death cannot bring it to an end. Only the body is affected by death, but the life of the soul is eternal.

The unity of a *chasan* and *kallah* is derived from the deepest level of their souls — it is an expression of their essential identity. For the souls of Israel originate within the *Kisei Ha-Kavod*, the Heavenly Throne of Glory, and there, in a realm above the world of time, each *chasan* and *kallah* are one. That is why, at a wedding, when the *chasan* and *kallah* are being reunited, we recite the blessing *"vehiskin lo mimenu binyan adei ad* — He [God] prepared for him [for man]...an *eternal* edifice." How can a Jewish marriage be described as an eternal edifice when a couple

---

55. *Zohar* I:85b.

can only hope to be together in this world for a finite number of years? The answer is that we are referring to the hidden unity of the *chasan* and *kallah*, to the unity of souls which the wedding merely reveals — and that unity is eternal, for it originates in a world beyond time.

AN AWAKENING FROM BELOW

Every one of a person's actions in this world has an effect on the higher spiritual worlds. In the words of the *Zohar*, "an awakening from below leads to an awakening above."[56]

In fact, there is a kind of symmetry between an act in this world and the response it evokes in the higher worlds. When a person gives *tzedakah*, for example, that small deed of benevolence will activate the infinitely greater powers of God's benevolence and mercy in the worlds above. Just as the act of *tzedakah* in this world gives sustenance to a needy person, so too the Heavenly response it engenders will be a flow of Divine sustenance to our world — a world which is also needy, in the sense that its existence depends completely on God.

The reason why the actions of a Jew can affect the highest worlds, the Ba'al Shem Tov[57] explains, is that the Jewish soul itself extends to those worlds. Every Jew is like the ladder in Yaakov's dream[58]: although his feet are standing upon the earth, his head reaches the highest Heavens. Thus an act of kindness in this world below can activate the Divine attribute of kindness in the world above.

The Ba'al Shem Tov quotes a *mishnah* in *Pirkei Avos*: "*Da mah l'malah mimach*,"[59] which is usually translated, "Know what

---

56. *Zohar* I:88a, III:30a.
57. *Kesser Shem Tov* 145.
58. *Bereshis* 28:12.
59. *Avos* 2:1.

is above you." On the simplest level, this *mishnah* is telling us to remember that God is above us and He sees everything we do. But the Ba'al Shem Tov discovers a more profound meaning in these words: If you want to know what is happening in the worlds above, if you want to know how Hashem is going to relate to you, you can know it *"mimach"* — by examining yourself. Hashem will respond to you in a way that mirrors your own actions and emotions.

We find the same idea, and almost exactly the same interpretation of this *mishnah*, in the writings of Reb Chayim of Volozhin.[60] He states: "Although the awesome and tremendous things that occur as a result of your actions are hidden from your eyes, you should know with certainty that everything which takes place in the higher spiritual worlds is derived from you, and it is directed by your own actions, much as an army is directed by a general."

Based on a number of rabbinical sources, Reb Chayim shows that the ability of a person to influence the higher worlds depends on his spiritual stature. Although even the actions of an ordinary person have an effect on the worlds above, the actions of a great and holy person have an effect that reaches the very highest levels of Heaven.

The *Avos* were so great that it is beyond our ability to comprehend their spiritual stature. They made themselves entirely subservient to God's will, and they were often accompanied by the *Shechinah*, the Divine Presence.

Hence, according to the principle stated by Reb Chayim, we can be certain that everything the *Avos* did on earth was

---

60. See *Nefesh Ha-Chayim, sha'ar* 1 (Bnei Brak: 5749), where the general idea is discussed at length. Reb Chayim's interpretation of the *mishnah* in *Avos* is in *Ruach Chayim* 2:1, and it is quoted in the above edition of *Nefesh Ha-Chayim*, in the section entitled *Likutei Ma'amarim*, p. 315.

mirrored closely by momentous changes in the worlds above. The deeds of our forefathers were not only a reflection of events in the higher worlds — they could also influence those worlds. Thus, even when the *Avos* were involved in seemingly mundane activities, their actions could affect the entire destiny of the Jewish people.

This is part of what our Sages mean when they say that *"ha-Avos heim heim ha-Merkavah* — the *Avos* themselves are the Divine Chariot."[61] Although this is a mystical idea that is not easy to explain in ordinary terms, in a general sense, it expresses what we have just described. When a chariot moves, it is directed by its driver and it is accompanied by its driver. Similarly, the metaphor of a chariot tells us that the *Avos* were completely obedient to God and closely attached to God, and also that the actions of the *Avos* both reflected and affected events in the higher worlds.

These ideas will allow us to understand why Avraham considered it so important to acquire the Me'aras Ha-Machpeilah. First, however, let us consider an aspect of the traditional Jewish marriage ceremony which might seem a bit strange, at first glance.

THE MACHPEILAH AND THE UNITY OF MARRIAGE

According to Jewish law, a marriage becomes legally significant in two stages. In the first stage, known as *kiddushin*, the *kallah* is designated as the future wife of the *chasan*, and for this reason the word *kiddushin* is often translated as "betrothal." In fact, however, *kiddushin* is more than an engagement, and in many respects the couple are already legally married at this

---

61. *Bereshis Rabbah* 47:6, 82:6.

stage. The second stage, which completes the marriage, is known as *nisuin*.

The laws of *kiddushin* are discussed by the Talmud in the tractate with the same name, and at the very beginning of the tractate *Kiddushin*, the Mishnah teaches us that money or any object of monetary value can be used to perform the act of *kiddushin*. This is the legal basis for the traditional marriage ceremony, in which the *chasan* gives a wedding ring to the *kallah*. Since the ring has a monetary value, it is valid for the act of *kiddushin*. The Gemara then explains that this halachah is derived from the Torah's account of how Avraham Avinu bought the Machpeilah as a burial site and paid for it with money.

At first glance, this seems very strange. We have many laws and customs that are designed to ensure that when a Jewish wedding takes place it is surrounded only by auspicious signs. We try to make every detail of the wedding a *"siman tov,"* a symbol of blessing and life, and we usually avoid anything that might carry a negative association.

For example, the halachic authorities[62] write that it is preferable to schedule a marriage during the first half of the month, when the moon is in a phase of growth and renewal. For the same reason, the *chuppah,* the wedding canopy, is usually set up beneath the open sky, under the stars, for that is considered a sign of blessing. Also, we do not make weddings during the days preceding Tishah B'Av, because, as the Beis Yosef explains, it would not be an auspicious sign. Similar examples abound.

Hence it is very surprising to find that the Gemara makes a direct connection between the laws of *kiddushin* and Avraham's purchase of a grave. It is especially surprising when we realize that, although in principle there are several valid

---

62. *Shulchan Aruch, Even Ha-Ezer*, 64:3, *Rema*; see also *Yoreh Deah* 179:2.

ways in which *kiddushin* can be accomplished, the universally accepted custom is to perform the *kiddushin* with money — precisely the method associated with Avraham's purchase of the Machpeilah.

It is also remarkable that the tractate in which we learn the laws of *kiddushin* begins with this reference to Me'aras Ha-Machpeilah. There is a general rule that "everything goes according to its beginning."[63] The beginning is a source, not merely an introduction, and everything that follows is derived from that beginning.[64] Hence the opening lines of a tractate provide a clue to understanding the entire tractate.

In addition, according to the mystical *sefarim*, every positive mitzvah is associated with a unique spiritual light. This light is revealed in the soul of a person who performs the mitzvah, and it can also be found in the tractate that discusses the mitzvah. Thus there is a deep spiritual connection between the mitzvah of *kiddushin* and the tractate *Kiddushin*, and, as we have said, the essence of the tractate is contained in its beginning. Since the tractate begins with a reference to the Machpeilah, there must be a deep and essential connection between the mitzvah of *kiddushin* and Avraham's purchase of the Machpeilah. This needs to be understood.

CONSTRUCTING AN ETERNAL CONNECTION

Avraham knew that his marriage with Sarah was a model for the Heavenly marriage between God and the Jewish people, and hence he understood that anything that would strengthen his own marriage would strengthen the Heavenly marriage. That is the reason why Avraham Avinu prepared a place

---

63. *Eruvin* 41a.
64. This idea has already appeared in several different contexts. In this chapter, see pp. 61, 73, 78, and 83.

where he and Sarah would be together even after their physical lives came to an end, and that is why Yitzchak and Yaakov also asked to be buried in the Machpeilah together with their wives.

In purchasing the Machpeilah, Avraham Avinu was acting to ensure that his marriage with Sarah would be permanent. Even at a time when all the outward aspects of their marriage had ceased to exist, even when, on a revealed level, the act of *kiddushin* which had united him with Sarah was no longer binding — even then, Avraham insisted that his union with Sarah endure. And by ensuring that his own marriage would be permanent, Avraham was also ensuring that the Heavenly marriage between Hashem and the Jewish people would never be broken.

Thus we find that the Machpeilah signifies the permanence of two marriages: the earthly marriage between a Jewish husband and wife and the Heavenly marriage between God and the Jewish people. When Avraham insisted that his union with Sarah be eternal, he showed us that a Jewish marriage is based on something deeper than what we can see in the physical world. On the revealed level, a Jewish marriage is limited to this world. From a strictly legal point of view, the act of *kiddushin* has a meaning only in the land of the living and not in the world beyond the grave. But within the Machpeilah, the *Avos* and their wives are united forever. And so the Machpeilah teaches us that a Jewish marriage is based on something more than the act of *kiddushin*, on something deeper than the visible world — it is derived from a hidden unity of souls.

At the same time, the Machpeilah ensures the permanence of the Heavenly marriage. The message of the Machpeilah is that even in a time of *galus*, exile, when Israel has been forced to flee from the bridal canopy of Yerushalayim, she is still united with her Beloved, *Ha-Kadosh Baruch Hu.* Even when Israel has been driven from her blessed, tranquil habitations of holiness and compelled to wander as an exile in foreign lands, she continues to be united with God in a profound and wondrous unity, just as in the earliest days of their marriage.

Although there have been times in history when it looked to the world as if Hashem had divorced His people, that perception was entirely mistaken. "Where is your mother's bill of divorce?"[65] the prophet asks. Since there is no bill of divorce, there is no divorce, and the essential connection between God and His people endures. On the deepest level of reality, the Jewish people is forever united with Hashem. That truth, however, is hidden from the eyes of the world, and therefore the place which expresses that unity, the Machpeilah, is also a place of concealment, hidden from the world.

With this idea we can appreciate a deeper level of meaning in the name Machpailah. The name is derived from the word *kafel,* which means "double." What precisely is doubled in the Machpeilah? Our Sages offer two answers:[66] (1) the Machpeilah consists of a cave beneath a cave, and (2) it is "*kefulah b'zugos*"— a place with "a doubling of married couples." This second answer is usually understood as a reference to the four couples who are buried there, but now we can see an even deeper meaning in these words.

Chazal are telling us here that the Machpeilah is the place of the two married couples we have been discussing. These couples are not pairs of individuals; rather, they are entities of a more abstract and general nature. The first is the earthly marriage, which includes the marriages of the *Avos* and their wives and also the marriage of every Jewish husband and wife. On

---

65. *Yeshayahu* 50:1; see also *Sanhedrin* 105b.
66. See Rashi on *Bereshis* 23:9.

this level, the Machpeilah teaches that a Jewish marriage is based on a timeless unity of souls.

The second married couple of the Machpeilah is the Heavenly marriage between Hashem and *klal Yisrael*. On this level, the Machpeilah proclaims that the marriage of Hashem with *klal Yisrael* is an eternal marriage which can never be undone, a union of lovers who can never be separated. Thus the Machpeilah is a place with a "doubling of married couples." It is the place of the earthly marriage and the Heavenly marriage, and it expresses the connection between them.

In light of what we now know about the Machpeilah, we see how profoundly appropriate it is that the law of *kiddushin* that unites every Jewish couple is derived from Avraham's purchase of the Machpeilah. Avraham bought the Machpeilah in order to ensure that he and his wife would be united forever, and his purchase shows us that a Jewish marriage is a *binyan adei ad* — an everlasting connection based on a unity of souls. Not only is there nothing inauspicious about remembering the Machpeilah under the *chuppah*, but, on the contrary, there could be no greater *siman tov*!

Buying a Share in the Machpeilah

Let us take an even deeper look at the traditional marriage ceremony and its connection to Avraham's purchase of the Machpeilah. Avraham and Sarah were the first Jewish couple, and so they contained within themselves the souls of all future Jewish couples.[67] In a spiritual sense, every *chasan* can be regarded as a part of Avraham and every *kallah* as a part of Sarah. In addition, the money that is used for *kiddushin* is derived from the money that Avraham gave when he bought the Machpeilah. Thus when a Jewish *chasan* gives the ring to the

---

67. See pp. 61 and 83; p. 89, footnote 64.

kallah for *kiddushin*, he is reenacting, in a sense, Avraham's purchase of the Machpeilah. The *chasan* becomes a partner with Avraham Avinu, and so at the very moment he performs the *kiddushin*, he is also acquiring his own share in Me'aras Ha-Machpeilah. Just as Avraham's purchase of the Machpeilah established his marriage as permanent and eternal, so too the *chasan* is establishing a marriage that is to be permanent and eternal — a *binyan adei ad*.

In this way, the money of *kiddushin* provides a link to the *Avos*. The *chasan* and *kallah* are reconnected to their source within the holy couples of the Machpeilah, and their own marriage, at its very inception, is united with the wondrous and holy marriages of the *Avos* and *Imahos*.

In addition, the *chasan* and *kallah* are reconnected to their source in the world's first couple, and that is why Adam and Chavah are mentioned in the blessings that are recited under the *chuppah*. "Blessed are You, Hashem," we say, "Who created Adam Ha-Rishon in His own image...and made for him [a wife] from himself [from Adam's rib], an eternal edifice [*binyan adei ad*]." Since our Sages saw everything with spiritual eyes, they understood that the *chasan* and *kallah* standing under the *chuppah* are connected to their source in Adam and Chavah.

Thus, if a *chasan* is worthy, he can accomplish with his *kesef kiddushin*, with the ring he places on his *kallah*'s finger, what Avraham accomplished with his four hundred shekels. He can make a marriage that is an eternal union and an earthly model of the Heavenly marriage between God and the Jewish people.

A Preamble to Marriage

The link between Machpeilah and marriage is also reflected by the location of these topics in the text of the Torah, for the juxtaposition of topics in the Torah indicates a connection between them.

In *parashas Chayei Sarah*, the Torah first tells us how Avraham bought the Machpeilah and then, immediately afterward, how Avraham sent Eliezer to find a wife for Yitzchak. The second *parashah* is known as the *parashah* of *zivugim*, matchmaking, since it tells the first story in Jewish history about finding a wife. (In Sephardic communities, it is read in synagogue on the Shabbos following a wedding, in honor of the *chasan*.)

Thus the Torah positions the *parashah* of Machpeilah as an introduction to the *parashah* of matchmaking, and now we can understand why. It is precisely the Machpeilah which teaches us the strength of the spiritual connection that is the basis of a Jewish marriage. The Machpeilah shows us that the connection between *chasan* and *kallah* is an eternal connection, a connection of souls that always existed and can never be dissolved.

LEAH AND RACHEL:
TWO SOURCES FOR THE SOULS OF ISRAEL

Jewish souls draw their life and being from the Divine Presence, which is often referred to in this context as *"Knesses Yisrael."* According to our mystical tradition,[68] *Knesses Yisrael* has two different aspects, and they are named Leah and Rachel. In other words, there are two different sources from which a Jewish soul can draw its life.

The first source is accessible to every Jew equally, regardless of his personal merit. Whether righteous or wicked, every Jew is connected to this source by virtue of his being a part of the Jewish people. This is the aspect of the Divine Presence called Leah, or *alma d'iskassia*, "the concealed world."

The second source, however, does depend on individual

---

68. See Rabbi Moshe Chayim Luzzato, *Sefer Ha-Klalim* 32.

merit, and a person's connection to it is commensurate with his deeds and accomplishments. This aspect of the Divine Presence is known as Rachel, or *alma d'isgalia*, "the revealed world."

A genuine understanding of these ideas is really only possible for someone who has been privileged to study the hidden wisdom of the Torah (the level of interpretation known as *sod*), and it is not for us to explain such deep and hidden matters. Nevertheless, there is a way to grasp these ideas with an approach that is somewhat simplified and necessarily superficial, the level known as *p'shat she-b'sod*, and it is on this level that we will proceed.[69]

Tikkun Chatzos

Almost every full-size prayer book includes a section known as *Tikkun Chatzos*. These are prayers that are meant to be recited at night, in the dark hours before dawn, and, according to the mystical writings, a person who recites *Tikkun Chatzos* with sincere feeling brings tremendous consolation and joy to the Divine Presence.

Tikkun Chatzos consists of two parts. The first, called *Tikkun Rachel*, is a lament for the destruction of the Temple and the bitterness of the exile. This part of *Tikkun Chatzos* is recited only on weekdays. The second part, called *Tikkun Leah*, consists of songs and praises, and it can be recited even on Shabbos and Festivals.

Based on what we know about the two aspects of the Divine Presence, we can understand the difference between these two sections of *Tikkun Chatzos*. The aspect of *Knesses Yisrael* known as Leah is the deepest root of the Jewish soul. It is the pure, enduring spark of holiness present in every Jew, righteous or wicked. It is a hidden point of purity beyond the

---

69. See *Derech Pikudecha*, by the author of *Bnei Yissaschar*.

reach of sin. This is the aspect of Chevron, the city that is invulnerable to *churban*. It is the aspect of *alma d'iskassia,* where the Supernal Union is never interrupted, and the marriage between God and His people is forever strong. Since *Tikkun Leah* refers to this aspect of *Knesses Yisrael,* it is a song of praise and a joyful expression of closeness to God, and hence it is appropriate even on Shabbos.

The aspect of *Knesses Yisrael* known as Rachel is the connection between the Jewish soul and God that depends on individual merit. It is the holiness in the Jewish soul that is revealed, and it is vulnerable to sin. This is the aspect of Yerushalayim, the city where the *churban* could have an effect. It is the level of *alma de'isgalia,* the light of revelation which allows for a possibility for darkness. Thus, in a time of darkness and *galus, Tikkun Rachel* is a song of lamentation and tears, and it cannot be recited on Shabbos.

WHY YAAKOV MARRIED TWO SISTERS

Yaakov Avinu, as one of the *Avos,* had an existence that our Sages describe as a *merkavah,* chariot. He was completely obedient to the Divine Will and constantly attached to God. Yaakov's deeds, like those of Avraham and Yitzchak, were able to reflect and influence events in the Heavenly worlds. In addition, however, Yaakov had a degree of perfection that made him different from all the previous *Avos.* He was the *bachur she-b'Avos* — the perfection and the crowning glory of all the Patriarchs.[70] As a result, the quality of being a *merkavah* was revealed in Yaakov's life to an even greater extent than it was in the lives of his forefathers.

This is what our Sages are hinting at when they tell us, "The image of Yaakov is engraved upon the Heavenly Throne

---

70. *Bereshis Rabbah* 76:1.

of Glory."[71] Only Yaakov is described this way, since it was in his life that the quality of *merkavah* was expressed most fully. In more familiar terms, we might say that Yaakov lived on earth and in the Heavenly worlds at the same time. More than with the other *Avos*, the events of Yaakov's life reflected realities in the supernal worlds, and the realities in the supernal worlds reflected Yaakov's life. What looks to us like two separate worlds was for Yaakov a single, seamless unity.

It follows that Yaakov's earthly marriage had to be a faithful reflection of the Heavenly marriage between God and the Jewish people. As we have said, every Jewish marriage has this potential, and in the marriage of Avraham and Sarah this potential was realized to a far greater degree than in the marriages of ordinary individuals. But since it was Yaakov who most fully expressed the quality of *merkavah*, his marriage had to represent the Heavenly marriage in the most complete and accurate way.[72]

The *Imahos*, the Mothers of the Jewish people, also had an existence which corresponded to realities in the Heavenly worlds. Rachel and Leah existed in the physical world in a way that reflected the Divine Presence, the Supernal Source of the souls of Israel. But the totality of *klal Yisrael*, in all its aspects, could only be represented by *both* Rachel and Leah. Either one by herself would only reflect half the reality of the Jewish people. Yaakov therefore understood that in order for his earthly marriage to be an accurate representation of the Heavenly marriage, he had to marry both Leah and Rachel.

Reb Chayim of Volozhin refers to this in his *sefer Nefesh Ha-Chayim*:

Yaakov Avinu understood that, because of the [exalted

---

71. *Alef Beis shel Rabbi Akiva*, s.v. *"vav."*
72. A deeper explanation of this can be found in *Zohar* I:72b.

level of the] source his soul, if he would marry both Leah and Rachel, he would be able to accomplish great *tikkunim*, rectifications, in the higher worlds.... That is why Yaakov was willing to work for so many years to marry both of them.

This is also one of the reasons why the Torah was not given to the *Avos*. For if it had been given to them, Yaakov would not have been permitted to marry two sisters.[73]

In his last comment, Reb Chayim is addressing the question of how it was permitted for Yaakov to be married to two sisters at the same time, a situation the Torah clearly forbids. Reb Chayim's answer is simple: in the era of the *Avos*, the laws of the Torah did not yet apply.

This, however, seems to conflict with the approach of the Ramban, one of the greatest of the *Rishonim*. The Torah reports that Rachel passed away in childbirth, just as Yaakov and his family were entering Eretz Yisrael, and Yaakov buried her in the place where she passed away, on the road near Beis Lechem. Why didn't Yaakov bury her in the Me'aras Ha-Machpeilah, less than a day's journey away? Given what we know about the immense significance of the Machpeilah, there must have been a powerful reason that prevented him. The Ramban explains[74] that Yaakov was ashamed to bring Rachel into the presence of his forefathers because he had married Rachel in violation of the Torah's laws.

But according to Reb Chayim, the laws of the Torah did not yet apply, and hence there was no sin. In fact, Yaakov's marriage to Rachel should have been his crowning glory, his greatest source of pride, for that was the step which made his own marriage a complete representation of the Heavenly marriage.

---

73. *Nefesh Ha-Chayim, sha'ar 1*, p.72.
74. *Ramban, Perush al ha-Torah, Bereshis* 48:7.

Thus, according to Reb Chayim's approach, we still do not understand why Yaakov failed to bury Rachel in the Machpeilah.

But even according to the Ramban's approach, we are faced with a serious difficulty. Yaakov was the most perfect of all the *Avos*. How could he possibly have violated a prohibition of the Torah? If Yaakov was later ashamed to bring Rachel into the presence of his forefathers, how could he have married her in the first place? Why wasn't he even more ashamed in the Presence of Hashem?

Permissible Sins

Yaakov had to marry both sisters, since that was the only way he could accomplish the great *tikkunim* Reb Chayim mentions. In addition, as Reb Chayim explains, the laws of the Torah did not yet apply, and hence such a marriage was permitted, strictly speaking.

Nevertheless, Yaakov was confronted by a problem. In keeping with his elevated spiritual status, Yaakov had accepted upon himself a higher and more restrictive standard of conduct. He voluntarily observed all the laws of the Torah, even though he was not required to do so. Yaakov, and the *Avos* before him, were on such an exalted level of holiness that they knew the commandments of the Torah even before the revelation of Har Sinai.[75] The *Avos* knew the spiritual meaning of each mitzvah and how it had to be performed in the physical world. Wherever possible, they kept the laws of the Torah precisely.

The Midrash tells us clearly that Yaakov observed the laws of the Torah even outside Eretz Yisrael. Upon his return from Padan Aram, Yaakov sent a message to Esav which be-

---

75. *Yoma* 28b; *Kiddushin* 82a; see also *Nefesh Ha-Chayim* (Bnei Brak: 5749), ch. 7, p. 202.

gan, עם לבן גרתי, *Im Lavan garti.*[76] The literal meaning of this verse is: "I lived with Lavan," but the letters of the word גרתי also represent the number תרי"ג, 613, which is the number of mitzvos in the Torah. Thus the hidden meaning of Yaakov's words is: "Even when I lived in Lavan's house, I fulfilled all the 613 mitzvos of the Torah."

Since Yaakov observed the laws of the Torah, he faced a dilemma. On the one hand, he needed to marry both Rachel and Leah in order to accomplish the awesome *tikkunim* we have mentioned. From this point of view, his marriage to Rachel was a great mitzvah. On the other hand, this mitzvah involved a kind of sin, at least in terms of the additional restrictions that Yaakov's refined spirituality had imposed on him.

As we know, Yaakov decided in favor of the mitzvah. He married both Leah and Rachel despite the slight "sin" involved. It is interesting to note that there are cases in Jewish law that present a similar conflict, and the halachic authorities rule in accordance with Yaakov's decision. Sometimes the Torah directs a person to perform a great mitzvah even though it involves a slight *aveirah* — although, to be sure, this is not a general rule of conduct, and it can only be applied in certain specific cases.

For example, the *Shulchan Aruch* rules that if a person has a very disturbing dream, he should fast on the same day, starting as soon as he wakes up. On Shabbos, however, it is generally forbidden to fast, since it is a mitzvah to enjoy Shabbos. But what if a person has a disturbing dream on Shabbos itself? The halachic authorities rule that he should fast on Shabbos. They add, however, that since he will be neglecting the mitzvah of enjoying Shabbos, which is a sin, he will have to fast again on a weekday as an atonement.[77] Thus it is possible for a person to

---

76. *Bereshis* 32:5. See *Rashi* s.v. *"garti."*

follow the halachah precisely, and yet to require a *kapparah*, an atonement, for what he has done.

Strictly speaking, Yaakov was permitted to marry Rachel even when he was already married to Leah. And it was a great mitzvah. Nevertheless, due to Yaakov's greatness, it also involved a kind of sin.

True, it was only a distant echo of the Torah's prohibition of marrying two sisters, but for the Machpeilah that was enough. According to the *Zohar*, the holiness of the Machpeilah was comparable to the holiness of the letters of the Divine Name.[78] It was a holiness so intense, so exalted, that not even Yosef Ha-Tzaddik could be buried there. As a result, even though Yaakov's marriage to Rachel was tainted by no more than an insubstantial whisper of a sin, it became impossible for Yaakov to bury Rachel in the Machpeilah.

Yaakov's Plan

It seems that when Yaakov first arrived in Lavan's house, he believed it would be possible for him to marry both Rachel and Leah without even the slightest hint of sin. Apparently, he knew that Rachel was destined to pass away before Leah — when Yaakov met Rachel for the first time, he wept, and *Chazal* tell us that it was because he foresaw, with *ruach ha-kodesh*, the circumstances of her burial.[79] He knew, therefore, that she was destined to die young.

The Torah's prohibition of marrying two sisters only applies when the second marriage takes place during the lifetime of the first wife. Hence, there was a way, theoretically, for Yaakov to marry both sisters, without any sin at all. He could marry Rachel first, and after she passed away he could bring

---

77. *Shulchan Aruch, Orach Chayim* 288:4.
78. *Zohar* I, 129a.
79. *Bereshis* 29:11; see *Rashi* s.v. *"va-yeivch."*

her to the Machpeilah, since their marriage would have been completely free from sin. Then he could marry Leah, and since this second marriage also would be fully in accord with the laws of the Torah, Leah too could be buried in the Machpeilah.

This was Yaakov's plan. Had it been successful, the history of the world would have been radically different. If Yaakov had succeeded in bringing both Leah and Rachel into the Machpeilah, the Heavenly marriage between Hashem and *Knesses Yisrael* would have been permanent with respect to both aspects of *Knesses Yisrael*. Not only would it have been permanent in the aspect of Leah, the hidden level; it would also have been permanent in the aspect of Rachel, the open and revealed level. Any separation between Hashem and *Knesses Yisrael* would have been impossible, even a separation on the visible level, and hence the entire exile could never have occurred. The Creation would have arrived at a state of complete perfection, as it will on the day when Hashem is known to all the nations, and His kingship is established throughout the world. On that day, *Tikkun Rachel* will be sung in voices of praise and jubilation, and the eternal connection between God and His people will be openly revealed, never again to be hidden.

THE WAR WITH LAVAN

As we know, that is not the way it happened. Yaakov was unable to bring Rachel into the Machpeilah, and he did not succeed in bringing the world to its ultimate perfection. What went wrong? The answer can be stated in a single word: Lavan.

Lavan was profoundly evil and extremely dangerous. *Chazal* tell us that he was the spiritual forefather of all magicians and sorcerers.[80] Lavan was the personification of an elemental force of evil, and he was driven by a stubborn, bitter, and relentless opposition to the revelation of holiness. His formidable spiritual powers were a threat even to a *tzaddik* like Yaakov Avinu.

Before Yaakov arrived, Lavan had never been defeated, and so when he made up his mind to destroy Yaakov, he fully expected to succeed. Lavan launched a war of annihilation against Yaakov, a war without respite and without mercy. As the *Haggadah* tells us, "*Lavan bikesh la'akor es ha-kol*" — Lavan sought to destroy Yaakov completely, and it was only Hashem's continual protection that enabled Yaakov to survive. When Lavan told Yaakov, "I have the power to do evil to you, but the God of your fathers does not allow it,"[81] he was describing how Hashem had foiled his plans, not only on that particular occasion, but throughout the twenty years when Yaakov had lived in his house.

Despite his power and cunning, and despite the vehemence of his hatred, Lavan was unable to annihilate Yaakov. Nevertheless, Yaakov did not escape harm entirely. In this respect, Yaakov's war with Lavan was like his struggle with the angel of Esav — the mysterious being that attacked him one night on the bank of the Yabbok River and wrestled with him until dawn. Esav's angel was unable to defeat Yaakov, but the Torah tells us that when the angel touched the hollow of Yaakov's thigh, Yaakov was injured.[82] However, it was not only Yaakov who was injured. According to the Midrash,[83] the angel's malevolent touch also harmed a number of Yaakov's descendants — righteous men and women who lived many generations later.

---

80. See *Targum Yehonason ben Uziel* on *Bemidbar* 22:5. See also *Yalkut Reuveini* at the beginning of *Balak*, s.v. "*va-yagar*," s.v. "*Balak hayah oseh*."
81. See *Bereshis* 31:29.
82. *Bereshis* 32:26.
83. *Bereshis Rabbah* 77:4.

Similarly, in his war with Lavan, Yaakov survived and even flourished. Nevertheless, he was forced to pay a heavy price. When Lavan succeeded in deceiving Yaakov — when he tricked him into marrying Leah instead of Rachel — Yaakov's plans for the future were thrown into disarray.

The problem was that as soon as Yaakov married Leah, there was no longer any way for him to marry Rachel in accordance with the laws of the Torah as they would later be revealed at Har Sinai. Yaakov could not postpone his marriage with Rachel until after Leah's death, because he knew that Leah would outlive Rachel. The only choice left was to marry Rachel during Leah's lifetime, and that is what he did. According to the Torah — the Torah as it actually applied to Yaakov — it was the correct and necessary thing to do. The great mitzvah of the *tikkunim* Yaakov would accomplish was more important than the minor sin of detracting from the additional holiness he had accepted. Nevertheless, his marriage to Rachel would now involve a slight transgression, and as a result, Yaakov would no longer be able to bring Rachel into the Machpeilah. The victory that had been within his grasp, the opportunity to bring the final redemption, had been suddenly snatched away.

Lavan had changed the entire course of history. What appeared to be only a minor delay — Yaakov would have to wait a week before marrying Rachel — was really a tear in the fabric of time that could not be quickly mended. Lavan had created a tiny gap in time that would stretch until it encompassed more than two thousand years of *galus* and a million tales of woe.

In a deeper sense, Lavan had created a dislocation in the structure of reality itself. Since Rachel, who corresponds to the revealed connection between the Jewish soul and God, would not be together with Yaakov in the Machpeilah, the Heavenly marriage of Hashem and *Knesses Yisrael* would not be permanent in a visible way. Thus there would be times when God's eternal love for His people would not be openly manifest. Lavan had created a gap between appearance and reality — and that gap is the very essence of the exile.

That is why, at the Pesach Seder, when we retell the story of exile and redemption, the *Haggadah* begins with the verse, *"Arami oveid avi va-yeired Mitzraymah* — It was an Aramean who tried to destroy my father, and he went down to Egypt."[84] The Aramean was Lavan who tried to destroy our father Yaakov, with the spiritual result that Yaakov had to go into exile in Egypt. And since the Egyptian exile was the spiritual root of all the exiles of Jewish history, the *Haggadah* is also telling us that it was Lavan who caused the entire *galus.*

Yaakov's Shame

A puzzle remains: Why does the Ramban say that Yaakov was ashamed to bring Rachel into the presence of his forefathers in the Machpeilah? Yaakov's decision to marry Rachel was entirely correct according to the Torah.

According to *Chazal,*[85] Yaakov was the *bachur she-b'Avos,* the perfection and the crowning glory of all the Patriarchs. Yaakov is the only one of the *Avos* whose likeness is engraved upon the Heavenly Throne of Glory, and Yaakov, more than either his father or his grandfather, was given the ability to bring the world to its ultimate perfection.

Yaakov knew all this. He knew, for example, that the *Beis Ha-Mikdash* that will be built at the time of the final redemption, will bear his name — it will be called the *Beis Elokei Yaakov.*[86] From this Yaakov understood that the powers that were needed to build the Temple and to perfect the world were powers that existed within his own soul.

---

84. *Devarim* 26:5.
85. *Bereshis Rabbah* 76:1.
86. *Yeshayahu* 2:3; see *Yalkut Shimoni* there.

In order to accomplish this, however, Yaakov knew that he would have to defeat Lavan decisively, and he saw that he had not done so. In one small but critically important detail, in switching Leah for Rachel, Lavan had outwitted him, and Yaakov recognized this as a clear sign that he would not be able to bring the redemption. Yaakov knew that he had been capable of bringing the world to its ultimate perfection, and therefore, when he saw he had failed, he was ashamed.

THE WEEPING OF YAAKOV AND RACHEL

The Midrash tells us that when Yaakov saw Rachel for the first time, he wept because he saw, by *ruach ha-kodesh*, that she would not be buried together with him.[87] Now we can understand the deeper meaning of this. It was not, as one might think, because Yaakov saw that she would die young, leaving a motherless infant and a young child. Although Yaakov had a deep love for Rachel, it was not for his own personal tragedy that he was weeping. When Yaakov saw that Rachel would not be buried in the Machpeilah, he understood that the Supernal Union would not always be revealed in the world. Hence there would be a time when his children would be driven into the bitter night of exile. That is why Yaakov raised his voice and wept. He was like a Jew who weeps in the dark watches of the night as he recites *Tikkun Rachel*, a Jew who weeps with pain and pity at the separation between *Knesses Yisrael* and her Beloved, *Ha-Kadosh Baruch Hu*.

A Vision of History

A second *midrash*[88] explains that when Yaakov first arrived in Charan, just before he met Rachel, he was shown a number of

---

87. *Bereshis* 29:11; see *Rashi* s.v. *"va-yeivk."*
88. *Bereshis Rabbah* 70:8–9.

sights corresponding to events in Jewish history. Yaakov recognized them as prophetic signs which provided a vision of Jewish history and the entire process of exile and redemption.

The first thing Yaakov saw in Charan was a well in a field. According to the Midrash, the well symbolized the city of Yerushalayim. Surrounding the well were three flocks of sheep lying down — these represented the first three of the four empires that would later oppress the Jewish people and drive them into exile. The Torah also states that "all the flocks would gather there," which was an allusion to the fourth and final kingdom, the empire of Rome, whose spiritual influence plays a role, even today, in the continuation of the exile.

Finally, just before Rachel arrives, the Torah records a remark made to Yaakov: "Look, his daughter Rachel is coming with the sheep," and here the Midrash quotes a passage from the book of *Yirmeyahu*.[89] As we read the *Chumash* together with this *midrash*, we see before us the arrival of Rachel and, at the same time, we can hear in the background the words of the prophet — and the sound of a woman weeping:

> Thus says God: "A voice is heard in Ramah, a voice of lamentation and bitter weeping. It is Rachel weeping for her children. She refuses to be comforted for her children, for they are no more." Thus says God: "Restrain your voice from weeping and your eyes from tears, for your work will be rewarded.... They will come back from the land of the enemy. There is hope for your future," says God, "and your children will return to their borders."

At first glance, the associations suggested by this *midrash* seem out of place, an interpolation rather than an explanation. Why should Yaakov's first meeting with Rachel be the occa-

---

89. *Yirmeyahu* 31:14–16.

sion for a symbolic vision of the four kingdoms that drove the Jewish people into exile? And why is Rachel's arrival announced by the sound of weeping? True, it is Rachel's own voice we hear, but why, for that matter, is it Rachel who weeps because of the *galus*?

As we know, Rachel personifies revelation, and revelation is susceptible to *churban*. Yaakov's marriage with Rachel was a model for the Heavenly marriage on the level of revelation, and it was Yaakov's inability to ensure the permanence of that marriage, his inability to bring Rachel to the Machpeilah, that led to the *galus*.

Hence, the two *midrashim* — this one about Rachel weeping for her children and the previous one about why Yaakov wept when he met Rachel — are really expressing the same idea. Both Yaakov and Rachel are weeping for the *galus*, for the suffering of their children and the pain of the Shechinah. And to both of them the Midrash responds with the promise of the prophet: "Restrain your voice from weeping and your eyes from tears.... There is hope for your future...and your children will return to their borders."

Inextinguishable Hope

One additional question needs to be answered about Yaakov's intentions. We know that when Yaakov first met Rachel, he saw that she would not be buried with him in the Machpeilah. But if that is so, why did he continue to search for a way to do just that? If Yaakov knew there would have to be a *galus*, how could he have hoped to bring the final redemption?

The answer is simple. Yaakov knew that a Jew must never give up hope. It is forbidden to despair. Even in the face of a Heavenly decree, one must continue to appeal for mercy, for a decree can be annulled.

And so, for seven years, while Yaakov worked for Lavan

and waited to marry Rachel, he was also toiling spiritually in a desperate and impassioned effort to nullify the decree. His exertions were tremendous. With his prayers, he uprooted mountains and stormed the highest worlds. He refined and purified himself again and again, continually ascending in holiness and *tzidkus,* and after each new ascent he would again hope that now he might be worthy to bring the redemption, that now, at last, the decree could be annulled.

This was also the deeper meaning of the *simanim,* the secret signs Yaakov entrusted to Rachel. The simple purpose of these signs was to identify Rachel on their wedding night, so that Lavan could not put someone else in her place. But beyond that practical purpose, there was a deeper reason. It is explained in the mystical *sefarim* that these signs had wondrous spiritual powers. They were the symbols of sublime *tikkunim* — works of spiritual rectification that Yaakov had accomplished in the higher worlds, and Yaakov hoped that the additional merit of these *tikkunim* would tip the scales in his favor and allow him to succeed.

THE DEEP COUNSEL OF CHEVRON

Even with the merit of the *simanim,* however, Yaakov was unable to annul the decree. Despite his years of toil, Yaakov did not succeed in bringing Rachel to the Machpeilah, and this meant that there would be a time when his children would have to endure the night of exile.

Let us now look ahead one generation, to a time when Rachel's first son, Yosef, was seventeen years old — for that was the moment when the darkness of exile actually began to descend. But even in that moment of gathering darkness, we can recognize the promise, the consolation, and the hidden power of Chevron.

After it had been decreed in Heaven that Yosef would be

sold into slavery in Egypt, a chain of events was set in motion to bring this about. First, Yosef was sent by his father to meet his brothers in Shechem, and the Torah writes, "*Va-yeshalcheihu me-eimek Chevron* — He sent him from the valley of Chevron."[90]

Rashi points out that there is something strange about this verse. Chevron is located in a mountainous region in the center of Eretz Yisrael, and when the Torah describes the travels of the *meraglim*, it emphasizes: "They *went up* through the Negev and came to Chevron."[91] Hence the word *eimek*, which means "valley," is puzzling. Noting this difficulty, Rashi explains that the phrase *"eimek Chevron"* refers to Me'aras Ha-Machpeilah and the *"eitzah ha-amukah,"* the profound advice of Avraham Avinu, who is buried there. (The Hebrew words *eimek* and *amukah* have the same root.) When Yosef was sent away from Chevron, it was in order to fulfill the Heavenly decree of exile that God had revealed to Avraham Avinu.

To appreciate Rashi's intentions here, we must remember that when Yosef left Chevron to find his brothers he was taking the first step of a journey that would lead him, and all of *klal Yisrael,* into exile in Egypt. Chevron, in other words, was the point of departure for the entire *galus.* And the fact that the *galus* began in Chevron was an *eitzah amukah,* a piece of profound advice from the hidden depths of Chevron — *me-eimek Chevron.*

It was God's Will that the *galus* should begin in Chevron because Chevron is the place that would give the Jewish people the power to endure the exile. It is precisely because Avraham and Sarah are buried in Chevron that we have had the strength to survive the exile, even to the present day.

---

90. *Bereshis* 37:14; see *Rashi* s.v. *"me-eimek Chevron"* (*Bereshis Rabbah* 84:13).
91. *Bemidbar* 13:22.

Chevron has stood by us in every generation, when the wicked have risen up to destroy us — for Chevron declares that even in a time of darkness and exile, we are still connected to God.

That is the *eitzah amukah* of Chevron — and it is a lesson so profound that it cannot always be revealed in the world. Hence it is hidden in the subterranean chambers of the Machpeilah, and there, in double concealment, in the depths of Chevron, there is no *churban*, there is no destruction, but only *chibbur*, union and attachment.

In fact, long before Yosef took the first physical step into exile, the very first announcement of the *galus* was made in Chevron. Hashem first told Avraham Avinu about the decree of exile at the *bris bein ha-besarim*, "the covenant of the parts,"[92] which took place in Chevron. Here, too, God's intention was the same: to sweeten the bitterness of the *galus* at its source and to mitigate the severity of the decree. Since the *galus* would begin in Chevron, it would forever bear the stamp of Chevron. It would be a *galus* based on, and tempered by, the eternal attachment that Chevron represents.

THE HIDDEN RESERVOIR

We have come to understand that there are two *Mikdashim* in the spiritual world, two sources from which we can draw holiness: Yerushalayim and Chevron.

When you think carefully about your own spiritual life, you will be able to identify times when you were blessed with spiritual illumination and clarity, and you could feel the blissful closeness of the Divine Presence. When you experience such moments of illumination and closeness in your own life, it means you have been privileged to ascend to your Har

---

92. *Bereshis* 15:1–20.

Ha-Moriah. There, as you stand upon "the mountain of God," you are in the presence of the *Avos Ha-Kedoshim*, and their holiness is revealed to you.

But you may also experience times when your heart is closed to all feelings of holiness and joy, and your mind is tightly shuttered. You sense that the light of Heaven is hidden from you by thick and gloomy clouds, and your eyes gaze upon a weary and oppressive darkness. You feel no desire for the Torah, and it seems to you that the gates of prayer have been locked, barring even the faintest beginning of a prayer. You yearn for your soul's Beloved, and although you search for Him, you cannot find Him. The trouble and the sorrow you feel are a sign that, for the present moment, your *Beis Ha-Mikdash*, your Yerushalayim, has been destroyed.

At such a time, when you cannot go up to Har Ha-Moriah, you must go down instead to the Me'aras Ha-Machpeilah that exists within you. Do as Kalev ben Yefuneh did, and pray at the tombs of your holy forefathers, who are hidden like a treasure in the depths of your heart. Pray, even if your prayer is no more than a longing for prayer. If you cannot make your prayer an expression of your heart, then let it be an expression of your faith. If you cannot pray with vitality, then pray with *emunah*. But do not desist.

Force yourself to learn Torah, even if now it tastes bitter to you, and you only recall with difficulty how its words once delighted you with the sweetness of milk and honey. Accept upon yourself the service of God, even if seems a heavy burden and you feel only weariness and indifference. Even if you can only force yourself to study Torah and to do mitzvos with a dull-witted determination, you must persevere, nevertheless.

Serve God with whatever powers you have *now* — with whatever you can find within your soul at the present time. If, for the moment, you cannot discover within yourself enthusiasm and joy, if the light of understanding is dim, then serve God even like the ox, who pulls forward steadily under the yoke, patient, resigned, and powerful. Or serve God like the donkey, loaded with heavy burdens, who is cold and lethargic, but also sure-footed, reliable, and uncomplaining. Serve God in whatever way you are able. But do not despair, and do not desist.

There is no place for despair, for your Me'aras Ha-Machpeilah is a wellspring of holiness that can sustain you even when the light of Yerushalayim is dim. Your Machpeilah can never be destroyed. The holiness of the *Avos* that exists within you can never be lost. True, it is hidden now — locked within the reservoir of your Machpeilah. But that holiness is waiting expectantly, and at a moment's notice it is ready to cascade outwards, to fill you with a revealed holiness and the radiant light of Yerushalayim.

In your time of darkness, take it upon yourself to fulfill the words of the Prophet Yeshayahu: "I will wait for Hashem, Who has hidden His Face from the House of Yaakov, and I will hope for Him."[93] Strengthen yourself continually with the *emunah* you inherit from the *Avos Ha-Kedoshim.* Cultivate *emunah* and nurture hope, for it is not the way of Hashem to reject any of His children forever, and soon He will turn to you again with great mercy and revealed kindness.

Wait for Hashem, with yearning and patience, as watchmen wait for the first light of dawn. Wait as the watchmen wait, knowing that the dawn must come, that soon the glory of Hashem will be revealed upon you, and in a moment the city of Yerushalayim will be rebuilt upon its holy place, and all its glory revealed.

---

93. *Yeshayahu* 8:17.

4.

GIFTS OF FAITH

YAAKOV AND ESAV'S DRAMATIC
COMING OF AGE

Parashas Toldos tells a story of blessings. It contains such an abundance of blessings that on the Shabbos when we read it in the synagogue, there is a blessing for everyone who is called up to the Torah. Each of the seven sections we read contains some mention of a *berachah* — either a blessing promised or a blessing fulfilled.

It is fitting that *Toldos* is the sixth *parashah* in the Torah, for the number six is deeply connected to the concept of blessing. Where there is blessing and bounty, we often find the number six and vice versa. For instance, when *bnei Yisrael* were blessed with a multitude of children in Pharaoh's Egypt, Jewish mothers gave birth to six babies at a time.

We find another connection between the concept of blessing and the number six in the order of the *ushpizin*, the Heavenly guests who come to visit us in the *sukkah*. According to the *Zohar*, the sixth of these guests is Yosef Ha-Tzaddik, who, more than anyone else, is associated with blessing. When Yaakov blessed his sons at the end of his life, Yosef was the only child to whom the aged Patriarch specifically mentioned the word *berachah*. And in the blessing

115

Yaakov gave Yosef, the language of *berachah* resounds and re-verberates: "May He bless you with the blessings of Heaven above, blessings of the deep crouching below, blessings of your father and your mother..."[1]

Even the name Yosef is related to blessing. It derives from the word *l'hosif*, "to increase," and increase is a sure sign of blessing. Indeed, Yosef's tribe experienced a unique kind of increase, for Yosef's descendants were counted as two separate tribes and thus they received a double portion in Eretz Yisrael.

The Maharal explains that the relationship between increase and blessing is reflected in the root letters of the Hebrew word for blessing, *berachah*: *beis*, *reish*, and *chaf*. Every letter in the Hebrew language has a numerical value. *Alef*, for example, represents one, and *beis*, two. The step from one to two is the most elementary increase we can imagine. It is the atom, so to speak, from which all other increases are built, the prototype for every doubling. Hence the letter *beis*, which we arrive at by going from one to two, represents the idea of increase and doubling. The letter *reish* has a value of 200, which is also a doubling, since it is twice the natural unit for hundreds — two times 100. And the letter *chaf*, which has the value of 20, is a doubling of the natural unit for tens. Thus the root of the word *berachah* corresponds to the number 222, a number with digits that are all doublings.

The name of the *parashah* also reflects the idea of blessing. *Toldos* means "children" or "offspring," and children are a fundamental expression of the idea of increase. The *parashah* itself revolves around two types of blessings: the blessing of having children and the blessings that parents give to their children. At the beginning of the *parashah*, twins are born to Yitzchak and Rivkah. Then, as they grow up, Yaakov and Esav struggle

---

1. *Bereshis* 49:25; see *Targum Onkelos* there.

over the *bechorah*, the birthright of the firstborn son.[2] Finally, at the end of the *parashah*, the Torah tells us about the blessings Yitzchak gives to his two sons.

Thus, *parashas Toldos* tells a story of increase and growth. Within that story, however, there was one fateful day that permanently changed the lives of Yaakov and Esav. It was a day of tremendous spiritual growth for Yaakov and a day of spiritual catastrophe for Esav. It was the day when their grandfather, Avraham Avinu, passed away.

A DAY OF MOURNING
IN THE HOUSE OF AVRAHAM

At the beginning of *parashas Toldos*, the Torah tells us how Esav sold his *bechorah*, his birthright, to Yaakov for some bread and a bowl of boiled lentils. This took place on the day when Avraham Avinu died, which is why Yaakov was cooking lentils. According to custom, a mourner's first meal after the funeral is provided by other people, and the meal includes a food that is round, like boiled eggs or lentils. A round food reflects the condition of the mourner, for what is round is closed, and the mouth of the mourner is closed by grief. Indeed, Jewish law prohibits a mourner from uttering words of greeting. Thus, at the beginning of the *parashah* we find Yaakov cooking a pot of lentils to give to his father, Yitzchak, who had just returned from the funeral of his own father, Avraham.[3]

While Yaakov was cooking the lentils, Esav came back from the field "*ayeif*," weary and fainting. Why was Esav so weary? What had he been doing? Esav's weariness had a spiritual

---

2. The *bechorah* is also a kind of *berachah* since it gives the firstborn son the right to a double portion of the inheritance and a special role in the service of God. Furthermore, the root letters of the Hebrew word *bechorah* are the same as those of *berachah*.

3. *Rashi* on *Bereshis* 25:30, s.v. "*min ha'adom.*"

cause — his soul was weak and faint because he had just committed the sin of murder.[4]

As the Midrash reports,[5] Esav had killed Nimrod in order to steal a precious set of clothing from him. These were garments with rare spiritual properties that Hashem Himself had made for Adam Ha-Rishon.[6] Esav coveted them because they would help him trap animals, so he killed Nimrod and took the garments for himself. When Esav returned home, his hands bloody and his soul weak, he was confronted with the news that his grandfather, Avraham, had just passed away.

Murder was not the only sin Esav committed that day. He also declared his disbelief in the principle of *techiyas ha-meisim*, the ultimate resurrection of the dead. This was the real meaning of his declaration ‫?הנה אנכי הולך למות ולמה זה לי בכרה‬ — "Behold, I am going to die, so why do I need this birthright?"[7]

The principle of *techiyas ha-meisim* is the belief that at some time in the future Hashem will bring the dead back to life. The souls of the righteous, which have been enjoying their reward in Gan Eden, will be returned to physical bodies in order to receive an even more sublime reward. According to the Rambam, it is one of the thirteen fundamental principles of Jewish belief. Hence, when Esav rejected it, he acquired the halachic status of an *apikores*, a heretic or nonbeliever.

There were other sins as well. As the Midrash relates, Esav committed five grave sins in the space of that one short day! Thus, the day when Avraham Avinu left the world was a turning point for Esav; it was a day on which he took a profound and dramatic turn for the worse. His latent wickedness burst

---

4. *Rashi* on *Bereshis* 25:29, s.v. *"v'hu ayeif."*
5. See *Bereshis Rabbah* 63:16 and 65:12, and *Targum Yehonasan* on *Bereshis* 25:27 and 27:15.
6. *Pirkei D'Rabbi Eliezer* 24.
7. *Bereshis* 25:32.

out into the open as he repudiated the sacred traditions of his grandfather and broke the most basic laws of human society. On that day, Esav emerged as a full-blown *rasha*, an evildoer.

REVERSE CAUSALITY

Why did this transformation in Esav take place on precisely the day when Avraham passed away? At first glance, we might think that Avraham's departure caused the change in Esav. In truth, however, it was just the opposite.

As Rashi explains, Hashem caused Avraham to leave the world on that particular day in order to spare him the anguish of seeing his grandson, Esav, becoming a *rasha*. Avraham should have lived to the age of 180, as Yitzchak did, but Hashem shortened his life by five years in order to fulfill His promise that Avraham's old age would be free from suffering.[8] In other words, Esav did not become a *rasha* because Avraham passed away. On the contrary, Avraham passed away on that particular day because that was when Esav's wickedness first became obvious to the world.

The Torah characterizes the brothers at precisely this point in their lives — at age fifteen[9] — in a most telling way: ויגדלו הנערים ויהי עשו איש ידע ציד איש שדה ויעקב איש תם ישב אהלים — "The boys grew up; Esav became a hunter, a man of the field, and Yaakov was an honest man who stayed within the tents [learning Torah]."[10] For the first time, the difference between the brothers was visible to the world. In their inner lives, there had always been a profound difference between Yaakov and Esav, but for fifteen years it had been almost entirely hidden, and

---

8. *Rashi* on *Bereshis* 25:30, s.v. *"min ha'adom."*
9. See the appendix at the end of this chapter for further discussion about the brothers' exact age at this moment.
10. *Bereshis* 25:27.

then, suddenly, it was clear to everyone.

But the Torah is talking about an even deeper change here — more than just the revelation of a previously hidden fact. By telling us that the boys "grew up," the Torah is hinting that on this day, the day they turned fifteen, Yaakov and Esav experienced a dramatic transformation in their inner lives as well. There was a change in who they really were.

It is impossible to understand why this transformation occurred without first being familiar with two basic concepts in Jewish thought. One is the idea that time is real, that it is a creation with a tangible substance of its own. The other is the principle that God maintains a precise balance between the forces of good and evil in the world.

THE DAYS OF A LIFETIME:
THE JEWISH CONCEPT OF TIME

We usually think of time as a way of measuring the rapidity of changes in the world. Time, in this sense, is measured by clocks and defined in terms of regular, periodic motions, like the swinging of a pendulum or the daily motion of the sun.

There is, however, a much deeper concept of time. Time is one of Hashem's creations, and hence it is as real as anything else in the universe. In fact, time as it actually is, the time created by God, has an existence that is similar in substance, and precisely tailored to, the spiritual life of every individual. Let us examine this idea.

What is a day? According to "abstract time," the time defined by clocks, a day is twenty-four hours — a stretch of time long enough for the sun to complete its daily orbit. But according to this, a day is only a length, a measurement, an empty space with no substance of its own. In contrast, according to "real time," the time created by God, a day is a piece of a lifetime. Time is the very medium in which we live; we are surrounded by time as a fish is surrounded by water. But time is even more than that: it is what canvas is to a painter, for time is a medium that records, with infinite sensitivity, everything we do and everything we are. According to the *Zohar*, on every day of a person's life, a new "day" comes down to him from Heaven. That day is like a blank sheet of parchment, and whatever a person does is inscribed upon that day. Then, as the day ends, it goes back up to Heaven, and a new day comes down.

That is the reason *Chazal* advise us to use the closing minutes of each day, when we recite the Shema and prepare for sleep, to repent for any sins we might have committed during the day. As long as the day is still with us, it is relatively easy to do *teshuvah* for those sins. While the "transcript" of the day is in our hands, so to speak, it is not difficult to erase and amend whatever has to be corrected. Once the day departs, however, it is harder to bring it back and to correct the record.

The same pattern is repeated with each larger unit of time. A week is more than a collection of seven days; it is an entity with an existence of its own. Hence, when a week comes to an end, it leaves us and ascends to Heaven. At the end of a month, the month goes up, and at the end of a year, the entire year goes up.

Just before each period of time leaves us, there is a short interval designated for *teshuvah*, like the time of *Kriyas Shema* at the end of the day. At that moment, we can review the entire period which is ending, and we are granted the extraordinary privilege of rewriting our own "transcript" before it becomes part of the "permanent record." During the week, for example, the time for *teshuvah* is *erev Shabbos*, and in the month, it is *erev Rosh Chodesh*, which is also known as Yom Kippur Katan, a "small Yom Kippur," since it is a time for repentance. And just before the entire year leaves us, there is *erev Rosh Ha-Shanah*.

Thus, the days of a person's life are an enduring reality. We see this from a statement in the *Zohar* about Avraham Avinu. The Torah writes, *"V'Avraham zaken, ba ba-yamim,"*[11] which is usually translated as, "Avaham was old, well advanced in years." The *Zohar,*[12] however, interprets this to mean, "When Avraham was old, he came with all his days." In other words, all of Avraham's days were perfect and complete; they were filled with mitzvos and *ma'asim tovim,* good deeds. Therefore, when he left the world, Avraham came before Hashem together with "all his days."

Each person creates the days of his life, one at a time. They constitute a faithful record of his life, an autobiography inscribed by his own actions. All of an individual's spiritual accomplishments are contained within his days. A lifetime of mitzvos and *ma'asim tovim,* every word of Torah and prayer, all the prizes he wrested from a recalcitrant world, the spoils of his struggles and the fruits of his labors — they are all locked within his days, like an immense treasure in a long row of strongboxes.

THE PAST REAPPEARS

As each day is completed, it goes up to Heaven where it continues to exist on a higher level of being. During a person's lifetime, however, his days are separated from him by a great distance, and their effect on him is weak and indirect. But all this changes — suddenly and dramatically — on the last day of a person's life. A short time before a person leaves the world, all the days of his life return to him. According to the *Zohar,* they come back in order to welcome him and to escort him upward to his place in the spiritual worlds.

At that moment, the past reappears. All the unremembered

---

11. *Bereshis* 24:1.
12. *Zohar* I:224a.

triumphs and tragedies of a lifetime return — bright, vivid, and real — and they take their place in a suddenly expanded present, a time without boundaries that is nearly impossible for us to imagine. It is as if the last day of a person's life stretches to include within itself all the previous days of his life.

For a *tzaddik*, the day on which he leaves the world is a day of unprecedented spiritual elevation. When his days return, all his mitzvos and *ma'asim tovim* emerge from the dim and distant past and suddenly enter the bright circle of awareness we call the present. All the spiritual light and energy of a lifetime is abruptly focused on the space of one small day, and the result is a tremendous intensity of holiness that can lift the *tzaddik* to spiritual heights that had never before been accessible to him.

Moshe Rabbeinu hinted at this when he spoke to the Jewish people on the last day of his life. His farewell address opened with the words "I am one hundred and twenty years old *today*."[13] With these words, Moshe was not merely stating his age. Rather, he was hinting that all the days of his life, all his 120 years of Torah and *avodas Hashem*, had just returned to him, and they were as vivid and immediate to him as *today*, as the present moment. "What I am now," Moshe was saying, "is much more than I ever was before. On every other day of my life, I was only accompanied by the spiritual accomplishments of that day. Today, however, I am accompanied by everything I ever accomplished, all the work of 120 years."[14]

As a result, Moshe was elevated on that day to an entirely new level of spiritual greatness. In describing Moshe Rabbeinu on that day, the Torah writes: " This is the blessing that Moshe, *the man of God*, gave to the Jewish people before his death."[15]

---

13. *Devarim* 31:12.
14. *Agra D'Kala, Vayeilech.*
15. *Devarim* 33:1.

This extraordinary title, "the man of God" (איש האלקים) is granted to Moshe Rabbeinu by the Torah only once — only on the last day of his life — for on that day he was much greater than he had ever been before.

A DOUBLE PORTION

In light of what we have just explained, we can appreciate a puzzling exchange between the prophet Eliyahu and his disciple Elisha. When the time came for Eliyahu to leave the world, he invited Elisha to ask for a final gift. Elisha responded, "Let there be, please, a double portion of your spirit upon me." Elisha asked for twice the *ruach ha-kodesh* and twice the spiritual greatness that Eliyahu himself possessed. "You have requested something difficult," Eliyahu told him. "But if you see me when I am taken from you, it will be as you have requested."[16]

If we think carefully about Elisha's request, we find something very strange. Consider a parallel case involving money. If a person had exactly one hundred dollars in his wallet, you could certainly ask him to give you or lend you the hundred dollars. But it would hardly make sense to ask him for two hundred dollars, since he can't give you what he doesn't have. How, then, could Elisha have asked Eliyahu to give him twice the *ruach ha-kodesh* that Eliyahu himself possessed? And Eliyahu's answer was equally enigmatic, for why should it depend on whether or not Elisha would see him as he left the world?

Strange as it may seem, that is the way it actually happened. When Eliyahu went up to Heaven in a chariot of fire, Elisha was able to see him, and at that moment, Elisha became twice as great as his rebbe. The Gemara tells us, in fact, that

---

16. *Melachim* II 2:4–12.

whatever Eliyahu accomplished in terms of prophecy and miracles, Elisha accomplished twice as much. But how was it possible for Eliyahu to give away more than he owned?

The explanation is as follows: Eliyahu knew that just before he left the world he would be much greater than he had been during his lifetime. Hence, if Elisha would be able to see him as he went up to Heaven — if there would still be a connection between them as Eliyahu began to ascend from level to level — then it would be possible for Elisha to receive his gift. To the extent that Elisha would be able to see the Heavenly Glory surrounding his rebbe, he would be able to receive a part of it for himself. And since at that moment Eliyahu would be many times greater than ever before, it would indeed be possible for Elisha to become twice as great as Eliyahu had been during his lifetime.

What happened with Elisha and Eliyahu also happened at other moments in history, when other great tzadikkim left the world. Devoted *talmidim* who were present when their rebbes departed also became heirs to a great spiritual wealth — an inheritance of holiness, an endowment of *ruach ha-kodesh*.

The Chasam Sofer refers to this in one of his sermons,[17] a eulogy in which he laments the passing of his great and holy rebbe, Rav Nasan Adler. He expresses his deep regret that he was not privileged to be at the bedside of his rebbe during his final moments on earth. If he had been there, the Chasam Sofer says, he would certainly have become twice as great as his rebbe. Such is the superiority of "real time" to our conventional model of "abstract time."

---

17. *Drashos Chasam Sofer, Drush hesped al Rabbo Ha-Gaon Rav Nasan Adler zt"l, Bereshis* 5561. Edited by Yosef Stern (5689), vol. 2, p. 742.

THE BALANCE OF POWER

We have said that there are two keys to understanding what happened to Yaakov and Esav on that fateful day. The first is the Jewish concept of time as real. The second has to do with the ongoing struggle in the world between the forces of good and evil. It is not generally known that in the course of this struggle, God carefully maintains a balance between the relative strengths of these two forces.

We see this clearly in the Talmud.[18] Rabbi Yehoshua ben Chananyah, one of the great *Tanna'im*, was often called on to defend the Jewish faith in public debates against the heretics of his time. Endowed with great intellectual and rhetorical talents, he easily refuted the arguments of his opponents, and he invariably emerged the winner in these contests.

When Rabbi Yehoshua ben Chananyah was about to depart from the world, his students became worried about the future. "Rebbe," they cried, "what will we do when the heretics come to debate with us? Who will do battle with them? There is no one to replace you!"

"You have no reason to worry," Rabbi Yehoshua told his students. "Even if there is no one with my talents, you will still be victorious. For if I leave the world, the heretics will also become weaker. They will never be more than a match for the best person you have to oppose them."

The Torah alludes to this, he told them, in Esav's remark to Yaakov in *parashas Vayishlach*: "He said, 'Travel and we will go, and I will go together with you.'"[19] The phrase "together with you" is a simple translation of the word *l'negdecha*. Looking more carefully at the word, however, we find two additional meanings. It can mean "opposite you," and it can mean "corre-

---

18. *Chagigah* 5b.
19. *Bereshis* 33:12. See *Rashi* s.v. *"v'eilcha l'negdecha."*

sponding to you." In other words, the verse is hinting that Esav's power in the world is always directed *against* Yaakov (opposite), and also that Esav's strength in the world is always matched by (corresponding to) the strength of Yaakov.

Rabbi Yehoshua ben Chananyah was teaching his *talmidim* that Hashem maintains a delicate balance between the forces of good and evil. Evil was created to allow the individual a freedom of choice, but in order for that choice to be truly free, there must be a degree of parity between the options. Hence the power of evil in the world can only be commensurate with the power of good that exists in the world at the same moment.[20]

AVRAHAM VERSUS NIMROD

This principle of equilibrium implies that if in one generation there is a great *tzaddik* he will be opposed by a great *rasha* in the same generation. If the *tzaddik* is on a lower level, then his counterpart will be a lesser *rasha*. But every *tzaddik* has an opponent who is precisely matched against him.

No *tzaddik* has an easy life, a comfortable, placid existence. The *tzaddik* is locked in a fierce, protracted struggle against an archenemy, a *rasha* whose strength and determination are comparable to his own. Whatever the *tzaddik* tries to accomplish in the world, the *rasha* tries to destroy, for the goals of the .*tzaddik* and *rasha* are diametrically opposed.

This opposition has been evident since the dawn of Jewish history. Avraham Avinu was the greatest *tzaddik* of his generation, and throughout his life he was opposed by Nimrod, a

---

20. This does not mean, of course, that God is indifferent to the outcome of the struggle. God's Will is purely that the *tzaddik* should vanquish the *rasha* and that every individual should choose good at all times. But by maintaining a balance, Hashem ensures that the choice is real and that the challenge is a reasonable one.

rasha whose platform was the mirror image of his own. Avraham taught that there is only one God, and that God is the ruler of the world. Nimrod, in stark contrast, proclaimed that he himself was a god, and he tried, through military force, to make himself the ruler of the world.

Avraham wanted to share his belief. He made it his business to travel from place to place in order to teach the world about God. Nimrod did just the opposite. He traveled through the world spreading disbelief in Hashem. *Chazal* tell us[21] that the name Nimrod is derived from the word *mered*, rebellion, and Nimrod's goal in life was to incite rebellion against the *Ribbono shel Olam*, the King of kings.

The ideological struggle between Avraham and Nimrod led to several direct confrontations. In Ur Kasdim, Avraham was arrested by Nimrod and thrown into a fiery furnace. Years later, Nimrod joined Chedorlaomer, the king of Elam, in an invasion of Eretz Yisrael, and their armies conquered the city of Sedom.[22] When Avraham heard that his nephew Lot was among the prisoners, he armed a small group of men and pursued Nimrod to the north, as far as Dan. There, with the aid of open miracles, Avraham defeated Nimrod's vast army, rescuing Lot and the other prisoners from Sedom.

At the beginning of *parashas Toldos*, we find a remarkable concurrence of events. On the very same day when Avraham Avinu passed away, his archenemy, Nimrod, was murdered by Esav. But now we understand that it was no coincidence. It was a direct expression of one the basic laws by which Hashem guides His creation. Since there must be a balance in the world, there cannot be a *rasha* who is unopposed by a *tzaddik*. If the *tzaddik* leaves, there is no longer any place for the *rasha*.

---

21. *Eruvin* 53a.
22. See *Rashi* on *Bereshis* 14:1, s.v. *"Amrafel."*

YAAKOV VERSUS ESAV

In the generation of Yaakov Avinu, the same pattern is repeated. Yaakov was the greatest *tzaddik* of his time, and his opponent was none other than his twin brother, Esav. In his generation, Yaakov was the principal agent for holiness in the world, and he always had to struggle against Esav, who was the principal agent for unholiness. Here, too, we find that Yaakov and Esav were buried on precisely the same day.

When Yaakov passed away in Egypt, he was brought to Eretz Yisrael for burial in Chevron. The Gemara[23] relates that just as Yaakov's sons were about to bury him in Me'aras Ha-Machpeilah, Esav arrived and insisted that half the cave belonged to him. Yaakov's sons reminded him that he already sold his share to Yaakov for a huge pile of gold and silver, but Esav denied it, and the brothers sent Naftali back to Egypt to retrieve the bill of sale.

In the meantime, Dan's son, Chushim, who was deaf and mute, became very agitated. Although he could not understand exactly what was happening, he saw that the funeral was being delayed, and this affront to his grandfather's honor filled him with a growing anger. When he realized that Esav was the cause, his rage exploded into action. He took a heavy stick and knocked off Esav's head. The head rolled down into Me'aras Ha-Machpeilah where it remains buried even today.[24]

Thus Yaakov and Esav left the world on exactly the same day. This was a fulfillment of the words uttered by their mother, Rivkah: "Why should I be bereft of the two of you in one day?"[25] On a conscious level, Rivkah was thinking only of the danger that Esav might kill Yaakov. But, as Rashi explains,

---

23. *Sotah* 13a.
24. See *Pirkei D'Rabbi Eliezer* 39.
25. *Rashi* on *Bereshis.* 27:45, s.v. *"gam sheneichem."*

she spoke with Divine inspiration, and the unwitting prophecy in her words was fulfilled years later when Yaakov and Esav were buried on the same day.

It was also a fulfillment of Esav's words to Yaakov — "*v'eilcha l'negdecha* — I will go together with you." Yaakov and Esav were destined to be always *l'negdecha*: opposite and equal. They lived their lives as matched opponents and balanced antagonists. Hence, when Yaakov left the world, there was no longer any place for Esav. The balance of power had to be preserved.

YAAKOV — WITH THE HOLINESS OF AVRAHAM AVINU

In light of what we have learned, we can now understand the dramatic changes that affected Yaakov and Esav on the day Avraham passed away, on the day when "*va-yigdelu ha-ne'arim* — the boys grew up."

Let us try to visualize the scene that was unfolding as Avraham Avinu prepared to leave the world. With his family gathered around his bedside, Avraham spoke his final words to each individual — words of blessing, instruction, and encouragement. Yaakov was certainly there, for he was an *ish tam yosheiv ohalim*, a man who spent his days in the tents of learning, close to his holy father and grandfather, who were his principal teachers. Thus Yaakov had come to Avraham's bedside to receive a blessing, to hear words of Torah, and to be with his grandfather during his final moments on earth.

Since it was the last day of Avraham's life, all the great and holy days of his life came back to him, days that were radiant with the brilliant light of Torah and mitzvos. One hundred and seventy-five complete, luminous, and majestic years of *avodas Hashem* came down to welcome him — and they were all present in that one small room. Avraham was surrounded by a terrific sphere of holiness, a *kedushah* more exalted and intense than anything he had ever experienced before.

In such an atmosphere of *kedushah*, a sensitive person, an individual attuned to holiness, would have been able to absorb a tremendous amount of holiness. Such a person would have received a great spiritual gift, just as Elisha did when Eliyahu went up to Heaven. And that is precisely what happened to Yaakov. When Avraham left the world, Yaakov's soul was filled with the tremendous gift of his grandfather's holiness, and he became a profound *tzaddik*.

ESAV — WITH NIMROD'S CORPSE

And where was Esav at that moment? To find Esav, we must look far away from the tent of Avraham Avinu and picture a very different kind of scene. This was the day of Esav's murderous encounter with Nimrod. Somewhere, at a dark, benighted spot in the forest, Esav chanced upon Nimrod, and when he saw the opportunity, he attacked and slaughtered Nimrod like one of the wild animals he was fond of hunting. Then Esav stripped Nimrod's gruesome corpse of the garments he so desperately coveted, and he took them for himself.

Thus, at the very moment when Yaakov's soul was being filled with a sublime holiness, Esav was bloodying his hands in a rapacious murder and dressing himself in the tainted spoils of his crime. As Yaakov was ascending in *kedushah* and *taharah*, Esav was defiling himself in the *tumah* of grievous sin.

But the impurity which entered Esav's soul at that moment was not only a result of the sin of murder — for the dead body that lay before Esav was no ordinary corpse. Nimrod had been the most wicked man of his generation, and the evil that he had committed during his lifetime caused his body, in death, to be an intensely powerful source of *tumah*, a stockpile of virulent spiritual contamination.

Nimrod had been the principal agent for evil in the world. A ruthless dictator, he had inflicted misery and death on thousands of his fellow creatures, and wherever his iron rule held sway, he had darkened men's eyes with a curtain of spiritual blindness. Through propaganda and indoctrination, Nimrod had waged a war to eradicate all belief in God. He had led a rebellion against God Himself, a war by which he intended to eliminate God's authority from the world — and to many of Nimrod's subjects, it looked as if he might have succeeded.

When a *tzaddik* leaves the world, all his mitzvos and *ma'asim tovim* come back to him, and the *tzaddik* is surrounded by an atmosphere of intense holiness. In contrast, when a *rasha* is about to die, all the *aveiros* and the *tumah* of his life return to him, and the result is a terrible atmosphere of evil and spiritual degradation. As his life comes to a close, the *rasha* is enveloped by a thick cloud of unclean and destructive forces — forces which our Sages describe as angels. Whenever a person performs a mitzvah, a beneficial angel is created, a spiritual being that acts to reward and protect him. An *aveirah*, on the other hand, brings about the creation of a destructive angel, a spiritual being that acts to punish the sinner, and can only be destroyed by *teshuvah*, repentance.

Thus, when Nimrod's life came to its brutal end and his wretched soul was about to leave his corpse, there were thousands upon thousands of destructive angels gathered about — all the hideous creatures that had been created by his foul crimes. They had come back to make a final, terrible reckoning with the dead Nimrod, to seize his soul and to inflict punishments upon it. Hoards of malevolent angels hovered angrily above his corpse, filling the air with the stench of *tumah*.

In such an atmosphere of spiritual degradation and pollution, in such a miasma of uncleanliness, what kind of person would be liable to suffer the greatest spiritual damage? What kind of soul would draw the *tumah* to itself as a magnet attracts iron filings? Precisely a person who had already set out upon the path of evil — someone like Esav.

For there is a general rule that holiness and unholiness are each attracted to their own kind. A soul filled with holiness will draw to itself any nearby sparks of holiness, and a soul sullied by *tumah* will be especially vulnerable to any unclean influences in the environment.

And so, as Esav stood by Nimrod's corpse, a terrible *tumah* descended upon his soul. It was far worse than all the *tumah* he had brought upon himself during the years when his sins were hidden. At that moment, Esav became a profound *rasha* — as we see from his actions in the hours that followed. Returning from the forest, he immediately declared his disbelief and sold his birthright. Since the birthright conferred not only a monetary benefit, but also the privilege of serving in the *Beis Ha-Mikdash*, Esav's contemptuous rejection of the *bechorah* was really a general rejection of the service of God.[26] Until then, Esav's wickedness had been hidden; from that time on, it was visible to all.

"ACCORDING TO THIS DAY"

Thus, on the day when Avraham Avinu left the world, a dramatic spiritual transformation took place in both Yaakov and Esav. Yaakov was well aware of the implications of this transformation, as we can sense in his words to Esav, when he said: "Sell me your birthright today [*cha-yom*]."[27]

On the simplest level, the word *cha-yom* means "today." But in a deeper sense, on the level of *remez*, allusion, Yaakov

---

26. *Midrash Aggadah* 25:32; *Zohar* I:228.
27. *Bereshis* 25:31.

was hinting at the dramatic transformation that had just occurred. The grammatical form of the word supports this reading, for the Torah could have written "*ha-yom*," which is the
usual way of saying "today." Instead it writes "*cha-yom*," which
means the same thing as "*k'ha-yom*," or "according to this day."
In other words, Yaakov was saying: "Sell it to me because of
the momentous changes in our lives which this day has
brought."

"My dear brother," Yaakov said, "since you are now so
tamei, so far removed from holiness and so distant from the service of God, what possible need do you have for the *bechorah*?
Sell it to me *cha-yom*, according to this day. This watershed day
of change and transformation is what dictates that you should
sell the *bechorah* to me."

TWO PHILOSOPHIES OF TIME

We can find an even deeper level of meaning within the word
chayom. In essence, there are two philosophies of life: that of
the *tzaddik* and that of the *rasha*. Although the difference between these two schools of thought is vast and far-reaching, it
hinges on a difference of interpretation regarding a single
word, the word *ha-yom*. In other words, the difference between
the *tzaddik* and the *rasha* is a difference of opinion about the
meaning of what we call the present.

The philosophy of the *tzaddik* is expressed by the verse:
"You shall keep the commandments and the statutes and the
judgments that I command you *today, to do them*."[28] The
Gemara comments on this verse, "*Today* is for fulfilling the
commandments, and *tomorrow* is for receiving a reward."[29] In
the *tzaddik*'s world, there are two times to reckon with: there is

---

28. *Devarim* 7:11.
29. *Eruvin* 22a.

a today and a tomorrow. *Today* — the present, every moment of our life on earth — is for doing mitzvos. *Tomorrow* — the world beyond the boundaries of the time, *Olam Ha-Ba* — is for enjoying the reward for those mitzvos. The *tzaddik* lives with a knowledge that the days and deeds of a lifetime have an enduring existence and that time is real.

The philosophy of the *rasha*, on the other hand, is described by the prophet Yeshayahu in the verse: "And behold joy and gladness, slaying oxen and slaughtering sheep, eating meat and drinking wine; let us eat and drink, for tomorrow we die."[30] For the *rasha*, the present is an opportunity to indulge in sensual pleasure. He is not at all concerned about the tomorrow — the world beyond time. In fact, he does not even believe it exists! For the *rasha*, every today is an invitation to enjoyment, and he believes that when the sun goes down the day and all its deeds will simply dissolve into oblivion. According to the philosophy of the *rasha*, human actions have no real significance, and time itself is empty and insubstantial, merely an invisible grid, an arbitrary frame of reference, a pale abstraction.

And that is what Yaakov told Esav: "We have two opposite philosophies about time. I believe that today is for doing mitzvos, and the World to Come is for enjoying a reward. You, however, believe that today is for pleasure and there is no tomorrow. If so, why would you want to spend your days in the *Beis Ha-Mikdash*?[31] According to your own philosophy, you have no need for the *bechorah*. Hence, 'Sell me the birthright *cha-yom*' — in accordance with what we each believe about

---

30. *Yeshayahu* 22:13.

31. Yaakov was not trying to encourage Esav to continue in the direction of evil. He knew, however, that Esav had already made moral choices that disqualified him from the *bechorah*, and he simply wanted Esav to admit it.

meaning of the present."

To this Esav responded, "Behold, I am going to die,"[32] a declaration of his disbelief in *techiyas ha-meisim* and an echo of the motto of his philosophy: "Let us eat and drink, for tomorrow we die." In other words, Esav answered, "What you are saying is very true. According to my philosophy, there is no afterlife and no eternal significance to human actions. There is only the momentary thrill of pleasure, and therefore, 'Why do I need this *bechorah?*' You are right; I have no use for it."

SPIRITUAL GIFTS

These, then, were the birthday presents the two boys received on the day they turned fifteen. Yaakov became a profound *tzaddik*, because he was present when his holy grandfather, Avraham Avinu, left the world. And Esav, in contrast, became a profound *rasha*, because he was caught in the whirlwind of *tumah* that descended upon Nimrod's corpse.

With this we can appreciate why the Torah uses the expression *"va-yigdelu ha-ne'arim."* Earlier we translated this as "the boys grew up," but now we understand that the Torah really means "the boys became *great*." (In Hebrew the verb can mean "to grow up," "to become an adult," or "to become great in some spiritual characteristic.") At age fifteen, of course, they were already adults in the legal sense, but that was the day on which they became truly great, "one in his wickedness and one in his purity."[33] Esav became great in sin and terrible cruelty, and his soul was filled with *tumah*. And Yaakov became exceedingly great in righteousness and purity, for on that day he received an immense gift, a priceless inheritance of holiness.

---

32. *Bereshis* 25:32.
33. *Bereshis* 25:23, Rashi, s.v. *"mi-mei'aich yipareidu."*

APPENDIX
Views of the Commentators
on Yaakov and Esav's Age
at the Time of *"Va-Yigdelu Ha-Ne'arim"*

In his commentary on *Chumash,*[34] Rashi understands the words *"va-yigdelu ha-ne'arim"* to mean that the boys became adults in the legal sense, and so he says that it refers to the day on which Yaakov and Esav turned thirteen. Until then, Rashi explains, there was little in their behavior to reveal the difference between them. As soon as they reached the age of bar mitzvah, however, Yaakov went to the *beis midrash* to learn Torah, while Esav went to worship idols. Thus, according to Rashi, when the boys turned thirteen, Yaakov became recognizable as a *tzaddik,* and Esav became recognizable as a *rasha.*

Rashi's approach, however, poses a considerable problem. To appreciate the difficulty here, let us consider the two possible ways of understanding Rashi's precise intent.

On the one hand, Rashi could mean that the outward changes in Yaakov and Esav took place on the day when Avraham Avinu passed away. If so, however, it is nearly impossible to accept Rashi's other statement, that this was the day when the boys turned thirteen.

The problem is one of arithmetic. The Torah states three ages explicitly: Avraham was 100 years old when Yitzchak was born, Yitzchak was 60 years old when Yaakov and Esav were born, and Avraham was 175 years old when he left the world. Based on these numbers, Rabbeinu Bachaye[35] and many of the other commentators conclude that when Avraham passed away Yaakov and Esav were already turning *fifteen* years old,

---

34. *Bereshis* 25:27, *Rashi,* s.v. *"va-yigdelu ha-ne'arim."*
35. Rabbeinu Bachaye, *Commentary on the Torah,* in his discussion of *Bereshis* 25:27, s.v. *"v'da."*

not thirteen.[36]

On the other hand, Rashi could mean that their differences were revealed — which he says occurred when the boys turned thirteen — some time *before* Avraham passed away. But this also presents a problem — it contradicts the *midrash* quoted by Rashi himself,[37] which states that Hashem shortened Avraham's life so he would not have to witness Esav becoming a *rasha*. According to this *midrash*, it is obviously impossible to say that Esav was recognizable as a *rasha* while Avraham was still alive.

Many commentators have pointed out this problem in Rashi's words, and a variety of solutions have been suggested. It is generally acknowledged, however, that none of the solutions are completely satisfactory, and one opinion even goes so far as to suggest that the number 13 in our version of Rashi's commentary is a printer's error, and Rashi really wrote 15!

Rabbeinu Bachaye[38] explains that since the Torah calls each of the boys *ish*, "a man," they must have been *at least* thirteen years old at the time, but he does *not* agree with Rashi's interpretation that the word *va-yigdelu* refers to the day they became bar mitzvah. Rabbeinu Bachaye follows the approach that events described in the verse "*Va-yigdelu...*" took place on the day Avraham passed away, and he therefore concludes, based on the ages recorded in the Torah, that it was the day on which the boys turned fifteen. This avoids all the difficulties in Rashi's approach, which is why we accepted the chronological reckoning of Rabbeinu Bachaye in our discussion.

---

36. Even if one were to suggest that the first two ages include additional months, it is still impossible to maintain that Yaakov and Esav marked their thirteenth birthday on the very same day when Avraham left the world.

37. See *Rashi* on *Bereshis* 25:30, s.v. *"min ha-adom ha-adom."*

38. *Loc cit.*

5.
THE ETERNITY OF FAITH
THE MIRACLE OF CHANUKAH

In the spiritual world, as in the physical world, there are laws. There are limits and restrictions on the way spiritual changes take place — at least in the normal course of events. For example, we know that there is a realm of holiness and a realm of unholiness, and the two are separated by a boundary. Since the creation of the world, light and darkness have existed as distinct entities.

We also know[1] that even if a Jew has fallen into a state of darkness and *churban*, the essential holiness of his soul remains intact. On a hidden level, his connection to God can never be broken. But what makes us believe that on a *revealed* level, light and holiness can be restored to such a soul? If an individual no longer wishes to return to God, how can we be sure that God will still help him to return? From where do we know that light has a power to transcend its own limits, to bring illumination into a realm from which it has been excluded?

The story of Chanukah provides an answer to these questions, but to understand it, we must first appreciate the

---

1. See chap. 3.

deeper meaning of the miracle that occurred on Chanukah, the miracle of the Menorah. The *halachos* that guide us when we light the Chanukah menorah provide a clue to this deeper meaning.

According to the *Shulchan Aruch*, all types of oils and wicks are kosher for the Chanukah menorah, even oils that are not drawn smoothly into the wick, and even wicks that do not maintain a steady flame.[2] This is based on the *gemara* that states, "Even oils and wicks that may not be used for Shabbos may be used for Chanukah."[3]

When it comes to the mitzvah of lighting Shabbos candles, we are very restrictive. We insist on a flame that is steady and smooth, and hence only the purest oils and the finest wicks are acceptable. The standards of Shabbos are very high. Chanukah, in contrast, seems to have no standards whatsoever. Even crude oils that burn with a dim, smoky flame, and coarse wicks that flicker and sputter — they are all acceptable on Chanukah.

THE LAMP OF GOD

When the Gemara speaks of oils and wicks, the Sefas Emes explains, it is also speaking about *Yiddishe neshamos*, Jewish souls. The lamp is a classical Jewish metaphor for the soul. *"Ner Hashem nishmas adam* — The soul of man is a lamp of God," Shlomo Ha-Melech tells us in *Mishlei*.[4] It has also been pointed out that the letters of the Hebrew word *nefesh*, which also means soul, correspond to the three basic components of an oil lamp: *nun* stands for *ner*, the vessel that holds the oil; *feh* for *pesilah*, the wick; and *shin* for *shemen*, the oil.

---

2. *Orach Chaim* 673:1.
3. *Shabbos* 21b.
4. *Mishlei* 20:27.

There are some Jews whose souls are filled with light on Shabbos. For them, Shabbos is truly *no'am ha-Neshamos, oneg ha-Ruchos, eden ha-Nefashos*[5] — an experience of spiritual bliss. When Shabbos arrives, they feel a sublime delight, and they are surrounded by an aura of *kedushah*. We could describe these *neshamos* as lamps that are lit by the Shabbos — a flame of holiness hovers over them and fills them with a Godly light. These *neshamos*, the Sefas Emes explains, are the oils and wicks that can be kindled for Shabbos.

Ideally, this should be the experience of every Jew. But unfortunately, there are observant Jews, people sincerely devoted to mitzvos, who complain that they don't feel anything special on Shabbos. Even at the time of the third Shabbos meal, when the holiness of Shabbos is most intense and the world is filled with a great yearning for God[6] — even then, there are Jews who look upward at the darkening sky, searching for three medium stars, waiting anxiously for Shabbos to end. These *neshamos* are like lamps that the Shabbos is unable to light. They are the oils and wicks that cannot be kindled for Shabbos.

The halachah that all types of oils and wicks are acceptable on Chanukah means that even those *neshamos* that cannot be lit by the Shabbos can be lit by Chanukah. On Chanukah they can experience the holiness and spiritual illumination they do not find on Shabbos.

How can this be understood? As the *Meor Einayim* explains,[7] there is a fundamental difference between Shabbos and Chanukah. Shabbos offers us the possibility of a great holi-

---

5. From the words of *Kah Echsof*, a Sabbath hymn by Rabbi Aaron of Karlin.
6. According to mystical literature, this is a time of extraordinary Divine favor, a time when God views, and responds to, the Jewish people with unqualified love.

ness that can bring us closer to Hashem. But the holiness of Shabbos is very lofty, and to enter this holiness we must raise ourselves to its level. Not every soul is capable of this, for it demands a high degree of purification and refinement. Some lamps have wicks which are too coarse for the holy fire of Shabbos.

Chanukah, however, is different. On Chanukah we do not have to raise ourselves to the level of the holiness. Instead, the holiness of Chanukah comes down to us. Hashem lowers Himself, so to speak, to each individual. He brings His holy fire down to kindle even the coarsest wicks — to illuminate even the lowest *neshamos* with a light that makes it possible for them to do *teshuvah* and to serve God with fiery enthusiasm and great wisdom. And all this occurs every Chanukah when we light the menorah.

BRINGING LIGHT INTO THE DARKNESS

A similar idea is expressed by the halachos that tell us where and when to light the menorah. For example, it is preferable to put the menorah in a low place, so that its lamps will be less than ten *tefachim* (about 35 inches) above the floor. Yet our Sages tell us that "the Shechinah, the Divine Presence, does not descend lower than ten *tefachim*."[8] Why, then, are we instructed to place the menorah there?

The intention is to show that Chanukah is different. During these eight days, the Shechinah does descend lower than ten *tefachim*, even to a realm which is normally too low for such holiness.

The other parameters of place and time connected with the

---

7. *Meor Einayim*, Chanukah. *Sefas Emes* 5644 makes the same comparison between *yom tov* and Chanukah.
8. *Sukkah* 5a.

mitzvah of *ner Chanukah* convey the same message. The Gemara instructs us to put the menorah in a doorway leading to the *reshus ha-Rabbim*, the public domain. We are also told to position the menorah on the left side of the doorway, on the side opposite the *mezuzah*. Both the concepts of a public domain and the left side allude to the realm of unholiness, the realm in which God's Presence and the light of holiness are not yet visible. Everything that acknowledges and expresses God's sovereignty can be described as a *reshus ha-yachid*, literally, "the domain of the One." In contrast, that which does not yet acknowledge Hashem's sovereignty can be termed a *reshus ha-rabbim*, "a domain of the many."

Similarly, the time for the mitzvah is evening, just as darkness is beginning to descend, and night is a time when the forces of unholiness are particularly strong. David Ha-Melech refers to those forces as wild animals when he writes, "You set down the darkness, and it is night, when all the wild beasts of the forest creep forth."[9] In addition, Chanukah occurs at the season of the year with the longest nights and the shortest days — the lowest, darkest time of the year. The final days of the holiday extend into what Rashi calls the "long nights of Teves,"[10] a time of both physical and spiritual darkness. According to some opinions,[11] in the year when the original miracle of Chanukah took place, the night of the twenty-fifth of Kislev was the longest night of the winter, and the following night was therefore *tekufas Teves*, a time that is associated with a particularly severe impurity.[12]

In such conditions — conditions alluding to the realm of

---

9. *Tehillim* 104:20.
10. See *Shemos* 27:21, Rashi, s.v. *"me-erev ad boker."*
11. *Toldos Yaakov Yosef, parashas Miketz.*
12. See *Regel Yeshara* (by the author of *Bnei Yissaschar*), Teves.

unholiness — we light the menorah. And in doing so, we show that the light of Chanukah has the power to transcend the usual boundaries of holiness and to penetrate even into the realm of unholiness. The light of the menorah radiates outward from the doorway into the *reshus ha-rabbim*, illuminating the darkness of the night and reaching down to even the lowest levels.

This idea is also expressed by the fact that Chanukah is a weekday holiday. We wear our weekday clothes when we recite *Hallel* and *Al Ha-Nisim*, and even when we light the menorah. On Chanukah, the light of Shabbos comes down to visit us within the darkness of the weekdays.

The word we use to refer to the weekdays is *chol,* which means "profane" or "not holy." It is related to the word *choli,* which means "sickness," and we can understand the reason for this connection. Something which is profane does not fully reveal the holiness that is the true source of its existence, just as the body of a sick person does not fully reveal the soul, which is the source of its vitality.

On Chanukah, however, the Shechinah comes down to visit us on the weekdays, as if to visit the sick. It comes to revive us within the darkness of *galus* and to restore light to our souls. Normally it is not considered proper for a great man to go to visit an ordinary individual. But there is an exception: for the mitzvah of *bikur cholim,* visiting the sick, it is proper. So too, on Chanukah, for the mitzvah of *bikur cholim,* the Shechinah itself comes down to visit even the lowest souls, and it brings them the healing and the light of Chanukah.

ON THE HORN OF AN OX

There is a reason why the holiness of Chanukah has this special quality, and it is connected with the story of Chanukah. To understand this, we need to consider the spiritual significance of the miracle of the oil and the historical context in which it occurred.

According to our Sages,[13] when the word *choshech*, darkness, is used for the first time in the Torah,[14] it refers symbolically to the Greek Empire. This, they explain, is because the decrees of the Greeks brought darkness to the eyes of Israel. As an example of such a decree, our Sages mention that the Greek government issued an order to its Jewish citizens saying, *"Kisvu lachem al keren ha-shor she'ein lachem chelek b'Elokei Yisrael* — Write for yourselves on the horn of an ox that you have no portion in the God of Israel."

Actually, the Greeks enacted many decrees in their attempt to restrict the practice of Torah and mitzvos. But our Sages cite this particular one as an example because it reveals the essential point of conflict between Greek culture and the Torah, the fundamental admission that Hellenism sought to wrest from every Jew. What Greek culture said to the Jew was "You must deny, ignore, and forget the fact that you have a portion in the God of Israel, and you must proclaim this denial in the arena of public life." This was the *choshech* with which the Greeks tried to darken the eyes of Israel.

But why did they specify "the horn of an ox"? And what exactly is the meaning of a "share in the God of Israel"?

Our Sages tell us[15] that the ox alludes to the sin of the golden calf, and that this particular sin, since it was the first one committed by the Jewish people after receiving the Torah, is a symbol for all the sins of Israel.

The Greeks were a rational people. But what logic could have led them to think that a nation which had entered into a

---

13. *Bereshis Rabbah*, chap. 2.
14. *Bereshis* 1:2.
15. *Vayikra Rabbah*, chap. 27, on verse 22:27.

covenant with God, and had maintained that covenant for over a thousand years, could suddenly be persuaded to announce that they were no longer connected to God? The answer is that they believed such an announcement could be made "on the horn of an ox" — as a consequence of sin.

When the Greeks looked at the Jewish people, they saw a nation which was, for the most part, no longer living by the terms of its covenant. Those Jews who remained faithful to the covenant were few and weak, and they were overshadowed in public life by a majority who were drawn to the spirit of Hellenism. Hence the Greeks concluded that the Jews would continue to assimilate and that they would soon begin to live like other nations, by the credo of "Let us eat, drink, and be merry, for tomorrow we die." The Greeks persuaded themselves that there was no longer any essential difference between Jew and gentile, and they thought their goal of creating a "Jewish culture" compatible with Hellenism would meet little resistance.

A GENETIC CONNECTION

Of course, the Greeks were wrong. And their error stemmed from their ignorance about the real nature of the connection between the Jewish people and God. The Torah describes that relationship in no uncertain terms: "You are children of Hashem, your God."[16] On the simplest level, this means that Hashem created us and cares for us with a father's love. But there are deeper implications. The connection between child and parent is based on more than behavior. A child's actions can reveal and strengthen that connection. But there is an essential, underlying bond which does not depend on behavior. That bond is an integral part of the child's identity, and it will always be a part of him.[17]

---

16. *Devarim* 14:1.

Similarly, the connection between a Jew and God is deeper than the performance of mitzvos. Mitzvos will reveal the connection and strengthen it, while transgressions will conceal it and make it weaker. But in the deepest sense, a Jew is connected to God just because he has a *"chelek b'Elokei Yisrael,"* a portion in the God of Israel. It comes to him as an inheritance from the *Avos,* and nothing can take it away from him. Even if he sins, that portion endures, and it will always provide him with a way to return to God.

As a result, the connection between God and the Jewish people is permanent. God is, so to speak, inextricably attached to the Jewish people — even when they have fallen.

A KOHEN IN THE CEMETERY

"How great is the love of God for Israel!" Rabbi Shimon exclaimed. His comment, recorded by the Midrash,[18] was inspired by the observation that when the Jewish people were in Egypt, they were on the lowest levels of *tumah*, impurity. And yet Hashem wanted so much to redeem them that He was willing to reveal Himself in a place full of *tumah* and idolatry.

To convey the significance of this, Rabbi Shimon offers a daring parable about a *kohen* whose *terumah* fell into a graveyard. *Terumah* is sanctified food designated for a *kohen*, and it is supposed to be kept in a state of ritual purity. A graveyard, however, is a place of ritual impurity, and so the *terumah* was already *tamei*. Nevertheless, the *kohen* was unwilling to abandon it. Under normal circumstances, however, it is forbidden for a *kohen* to enter a graveyard, and so the *kohen* was faced with a dilemma.

"What shall I do?" the *kohen* wondered. "If I go into the

---

17. See chap. 1, pp. 10, 25.
18. *Shemos Rabbah* 15:6.

graveyard, I will become *tamei*, and that is impossible. But to leave my *terumah* there is also impossible!"

The *kohen* finally decided, "It is better to save my *terumah*, even if I will become impure. For I can become pure again later. But if I lose my *terumah*, it will be lost to me forever."

The *kohen* in the parable represents Hashem and the *terumah* represents the Jewish people. The message is twofold. First, Hashem is unwilling to separate Himself from the Jewish people, even when they have fallen. And second, Hashem is ready to rescue them, even if it means He must bring His holiness down to a level where it cannot usually go, just as a *kohen* is not usually permitted to enter a cemetery.

HIDDEN POINT OF HOLINESS

When the Greeks entered the *Beis Ha-Mikdash*, they defiled all the oils they found there. One small flask of oil, however, remained beyond their reach. Deeply hidden, protected by the seal of the *kohen gadol*, this flask remained entirely pure. Later, when it was discovered by the Chashmonaim, this small flask made it possible to relight the Menorah in a state of complete purity. Then it burned miraculously for eight days, allowing the Menorah to continue to give its light on the same level of purity, without interruption.

Similarly, deeply hidden within the heart of every Jew there is a point of complete purity. Concealed beyond the reach of any foreign influences, invulnerable to *churban* and protected from all *tumah*, this point contains within itself the unblemished holiness that a Jew inherits from the *Avos*.

Even in a Jew who has fallen very low and whose outward appearance fails to reveal the faintest glimmer of holiness, this hidden point of holiness endures. It may be invisible — but it is indestructible. If such a Jew will only make up his mind to return to Hashem, this hidden point will permit him to "rededicate his house" in purity, and it will illuminate his being with a revealed and perceptible holiness. This invisible reservoir of holiness is the *"chelek b'Elokei Yisrael"* that belongs to every Jew, and it is the spiritual reality to which the miracle of the flask of oil attests.

This is the lesson of Chanukah and the source of our obligation to give thanks. When a Jew lights the menorah on Chanukah, he is making a declaration that despite all his failings, and despite the level to which he has fallen, he still possesses a *"chelek b'Elokei Yisrael."* By lighting the menorah he shows that even when he no longer has the power to raise himself up, the Shechinah will come down to where he is — and in that darkness, the Shechinah will illuminate him with its holy light.

SHABBOS AND CHANUKAH, SHEMITTAH AND YOVEL

The Maharal[19] provides us with an additional insight into the essential difference between Shabbos and Chanukah. We celebrate Shabbos because God's creation of the world was completed on the seventh day. The holiness of Shabbos is therefore related to the number seven, and the number seven is related to natural order. The holiness of Chanukah, however, is rooted in the number eight, which is why the miracle of Chanukah lasted for eight days. And the number eight, being the next number higher than seven, always refers to that which is higher than nature, to the realm of the miraculous.

Since the Torah is higher than nature, it is also connected with the number eight. That is why the Torah was given exactly fifty days after the Exodus from Egypt, for the fiftieth day is the beginning of the eighth week.

---

19. *Ner Mitzvah*, pp. 22-23 (Bnei Brak: *Yahadus* 5732).

The Maharal goes on to explain that the two inner rooms of the *Beis Ha-Mikdash* also had a holiness that was related to the numbers seven and eight. If one entered the central building of the *Beis Ha-Mikdash* and walked towards the west, one would enter the *Heichal*, the Sanctuary, where the Menorah stood. The Menorah's spiritual function was to reveal the light of holiness and Torah to the world, and the fact that it had seven branches means that its holiness, and that of the *Heichal*, was related to the number seven.

To the west of the *Heichal* was the *Kodesh Ha-Kodashim*, the Holy of Holies. This was the innermost chamber of the *Beis Ha-Mikdash* and the location of the *Aron Kodesh*, which contained the Tablets of the Law. In the *Kodesh Ha-Kodashim* the laws of the physical world were suspended, as we see clearly from a discussion in the Gemara[20] about the dimensions of the *Aron Kodesh*. The *Aron* was a physical object with its own precise dimensions. Nevertheless, if one measured from the two sides of the *Aron* to the opposite walls of the room, the sum of the two numbers would always be equal to the full width of the room, as if the *Aron* did not take up any space at all — an obvious contradiction to the laws of geometry. Thus the Holy of Holies was a place above the laws of nature, and therefore it had a connection with the number eight.

The function of the Menorah was to reveal the light of holiness and Torah to the world. But the Maharal tells us that the true source of the Menorah's light — the hidden wellspring from which its light flowed — was the *Kodesh Ha-Kodashim*. We can appreciate this when we realize that the *Kodesh Ha-Kodashim* was the place of the Shechinah, the source of the holiness, and it was also the location of the Tablets of the Law, the source of the Torah.

---

20. *Megillah* 10b.

When the Greeks entered the *Heichal*, they were able to defile the Menorah with its seven branches. But in the *Kodesh Ha-Kodashim*, the Maharal explains, the Greeks had no power at all to affect the holiness. Hence the source of the light was never profaned, and so, when the Chashmonaim returned to the Temple and relit the Menorah, it was possible to restore the original light and holiness from this higher level.

Thus, the source of the miracle of Chanukah is a very high level of holiness, one which is hidden beyond the reach of *tumah*, and from that level, holiness and purity can be restored to the lower levels. That is why Chanukah, even today, has the ability to restore the light of holiness to the lowest *neshamos*.

In this context, we may add that there is a similar contrast between the numbers seven and eight in the two special years that bring freedom to a Jewish slave, an *eved Ivri*. If a Jew becomes a slave, he experiences a decline in *kedushah*, and this change is reflected in the *halachos* that govern his status. A Jew is normally forbidden to marry a non-Jewish woman, but if he becomes a slave, there are circumstances in which he is allowed to live with a non-Jewish female slave.

Hence, on the homiletical level (*d'rash*), the *eved Ivri* is a metaphor for Jews who have experienced a spiritual decline, and the laws pertaining to the *eved Ivri* can also be understood in this light. The Torah tells us, for example, that an *eved Ivri* is not required to work for more than six years, and in the seventh year he is allowed to go free.[21] Just as the laws of *shemittah* require a cessation of agricultural labor in the Land of Israel every seventh year, so too, the Torah grants the *eved Ivri* a kind of personal *shemittah*, and after six years of work he is allowed to return to the status of a free man.

The Torah goes on to mention, however, that if an *eved Ivri*

---

21. *Shemos* 21:2.

does not want to leave his master or his non-Jewish wife, he may choose to remain in servitude even after the beginning of the seventh year.[22] On the homiletical level, the Torah is referring to souls who have fallen so low that they no longer wish to free themselves from the *tumah* to which they have become accustomed. For such Jews, the light of Shabbos, which is related to the number seven, can no longer restore their souls to a state of holiness.

Nevertheless, the Torah provides a remedy even for such entangled souls. Although an *eved Ivri* may refuse to accept his freedom in the seventh year, the Torah promises us that he will not remain a slave indefinitely. When the Jewish people finish counting seven *shemittah* cycles and the fiftieth year arrives — the year known as *yovel* — every *eved Ivri*, without exception, must go free. On the homiletical level, this means that Hashem will provide a force from above, a powerful spiritual illumination which will propel those souls beyond their own limitations, and in this way even the most recalcitrant souls will be restored to holiness.

The special power of *yovel* is related to the number eight. Since it is the fiftieth year, it is the beginning of the eighth *shemittah* cycle, and hence it is rooted in the world above nature, the world of the miraculous. That is why the *yovel* has the power to free even the lowest *neshamos* and to return them to their rightful inheritance.

Because Chanukah is rooted in the number eight, it also has a power like that of *yovel*, the power to restore holiness to even the lowest *neshamos*. And that is why the light of Chanukah is able to illuminate even the souls that cannot respond to the holiness of Shabbos.

---

22. *Shemos* 41:5.

LIGHT FROM THE DARKNESS

The miracle of Chanukah took place in several stages, and if we look carefully, we find that each of them illustrates an aspect of faith we have discussed earlier. The first stage of the miracle took place when the Greeks were unable to defile all the oil in the *Beis Ha-Mikdash*. As the Maharal explains, this was because the deepest level of holiness, the holiness of the *Kodesh Ha-Kodashim,* was beyond the reach of *tumah.* This corresponds to the fact that even if a Jew has fallen into a state of *churban* and defilement, the deepest aspect of his soul remains entirely pure. Within the Jewish heart there is a hidden point of purity, a Machpeilah, where the soul is permanently connected to God.[23] The invulnerability of this aspect of the soul is not so much a miracle as a fact — it exists on a level that is far beyond any interference by the forces of the world.

A second aspect of the miracle was the *nisayon* faced by the Chashmonaim. A "realistic" evaluation of their situation would have convinced them that it was impossible to fulfill God's commandments regarding the *Beis Ha-Mikdash*. Yet they did not resign themselves to the "inevitable," and they did not despair. Like Avraham Avinu at the *akeidah*, they strengthened themselves with a faith that was pure and unquestioning.[24] They devoted themselves to fulfilling God's will, and they set aside all personal considerations. Although they were forced to act in a situation of darkness, they arrived, in the end, at a great light. Ignoring the arguments of doubt, they were rewarded with the holiday of Chanukah, an eternal reminder of the power and purity of faith.

The next stage of the miracle took place when the Chashmonaim found the small flask of pure oil and used it to

---

23. See chap. 3.
24. See chap. 2.

relight the Menorah. This corresponds to the fact that the hidden point of purity is not only eternal but can also be recovered and revealed. A Jew has a hereditary belief in God, a knowledge derived from the deepest level of his being.[25] It is a knowledge that can be forgotten and concealed, and in some individuals it may be entirely unconscious, but even then it can be recovered and revealed.

The most famous aspect of the miracle of Chanukah is the fact that the small quantity of pure oil burned for eight days. Since the number eight refers to a level above nature and time, this means that the oil gave light in a way that was above the limitations of nature and time. As the Maharal explains, the miracle of Chanukah came from the *Kodesh Ha-Kodashim*, a place characterized by the number eight, and hence it was also revealed in the world in a manner characterized by the number eight.

We already know that the hidden point of purity in the Jewish soul is unaffected by the vicissitudes of time. The miracle of the Menorah, however, shows us something even more remarkable: even when that timeless point of holiness is revealed in the world, it continues to transcend the limits of time and space. When the Chashmonaim lit the Menorah and it burned for eight days, the limits of time were transcended.[26] And each year when we light the Chanukah menorah, the normal limits of "spiritual space" — the barriers between higher

---

25. See chap. 1.
26. There are many different explanations about what precisely the Chashmonaim did when they lit the Menorah, and why we consider the miracle to have lasted for eight days. One explanation is that there was a miraculous change not in the nature of the oil, but in the way that time itself was operating in the *Beis Ha-Mikdash*. This is related to the idea presented in chap. 4, that time has a reality that cannot be measured by the hands of a clock.

and lower — are also suspended. The Shechinah descends lower than ten *tefachim*, and the light of Chanukah reaches into the darkness, bringing holiness to the very lowest levels.

The general lesson of Chanukah is that even in a time of darkness, Hashem does not abandon the Jewish people, and this applies to each individual Jew as well. Chanukah shows us that a time of trial and darkness can lead to a rediscovery of the *chelek be'Elokei Yisrael* and a new revelation of the faith that is hidden in the Jewish heart. And when that faith is revealed, the darkness is filled with a light that transcends the limits of time and nature, a light that reveals the eternity of faith itself.

The lessons of Chanukah also apply to the overall shape of world history. In this sense, Chanukah hints at the goal toward which all of history is constantly moving, the final and complete Redemption. Like the miracle of Chanukah, the Redemption will come as a result of the faithfulness of the Jewish people amidst the trials of *galus*, and with its arrival, the darkness of *galus* will be replaced by the brilliant light of *geulah*. Like the light of Chanukah, the light of *geulah* will be a light beyond the limits of time and nature, and it will bring holiness to even the lowest levels. The hidden point of purity in every Jewish soul will be revealed, and "the earth will be filled with the knowledge of God, as the waters fill the ocean."[27] May it be speedily and in our days!

---

27. *Yeshayahu* 11:9; see *Mishnah Torah, Hilchos Melachim* 12:5.

Glossary

The following glossary provides a partial explanation of some of the Hebrew, Yiddish (Y.) and Aramaic (A.) words and phrases used in this book. The spellings and explanations reflect the way the specific word is used herein. Often there are alternate spellings and meanings for the words.

AKEIDAH: Avraham's binding of Yitzchak on the altar.

AL HA-NISIM: a thanksgiving prayer for miracles, added to the prayer service and the Grace after Meals on Chanukah and Purim.

AL KIDDUSH HASHEM: sanctification of the Divine Name; martyrdom.

ALEF: the first letter of the Hebrew alphabet.

ALIYAH L'REGEL: pilgrimage to the Holy Temple in Jerusalem.

APIKORSUS: heresy.

ARON KODESH: the Holy Ark in the Temple. It contained the fragments of the Tablets of the Law that were received at Mount Sinai.

AV: the Hebrew month corresponding to July/August.

AVEIRAH: a transgression.

AVODAS HASHEM: the service of God through Torah study, mitzvos, and prayer, or any other activity performed in a true spirit of worship.

AVODAH ZARAH: idolatry.

AVOS: the Patriarchs.

BECHORAH: the birthright.

BEIS: the second letter of the Hebrew alphabet.

BEIS HA-MIKDASH: the Holy Temple.

BEIS MIDRASH: the study hall of a yeshivah.

BERACHAH: a blessing.

BIKUR CHOLIM: the mitzvah of visiting the sick.

BNEI YISRAEL: the Children of Israel, i.e. the Jewish People.

CHASAN: a bridegroom.

CHAZAL: the Hebrew acronym for "our Sages, of blessed memory."

CHEDER: lit., "room"; (Y.) a religious primary school for boys.

CHESSED: loving-kindness; compassion.
CHOSHECH: darkness.
CHUMASH: [one of] the Five Books of Moses.
CHUPPAH: the wedding canopy; (colloq.) a wedding.
CHURBAN: destruction; the Destruction of the Holy Temple in Jerusalem.

DIN: the Divine attribute of strict justice.

EMUNAH: belief in God; faith.
EMUNAH PESHUTAH: simple faith.
EREV ROSH CHODESH: the day preceding Rosh Chodesh.
EREV ROSH HA-SHANAH: the day preceding Rosh Hashanah.
EREV SHABBOS: the day preceding the Sabbath, i.e. Friday.
EVED IVRI: a Hebrew slave.
EVEN SHESIYAH: "the foundation stone," the large stone that was located under the Holy of Holies in the Temple.

GA'AVAH: pride, egotism, arrogance.
GALUS: exile.

HAFTARAH: a passage from the Prophetic writings, read after the Torah reading in the synagogue on the Sabbath.
HA-KADOSH BARUCH HU: the Holy One blessed be He (God).
HALLEL: psalms of praise (*Tehillim* 113–118) recited on Rosh Chodesh and Festivals.
HEH: the fifth letter fo the Hebrew alphabet.

IKVESA D'MESHICHA: (A.) lit., "the footsteps of the Messiah"; that is, the period immediately preceding the arrival of the Messiah.
IMAHOS: the Matriarchs.

KALLAH: a bride.
KEDUSHAH: holiness.
KIBBUD AV: the commandment to honor one's father.
KISEI HA-KAVOD: God's Throne of Glory.
KLAL YISRAEL: the community of the people of Israel; the Jewish Nation.
KODESH HA-KODASHIM: the Holy of Holies.
KOHEN: a member fo the priestly order, a direct descendant of Aharon the first High Priest.
KOHEN GADOL: the High Priest.
KRIAS SHEMA: recitation of the *Shema* prayer.

LESHON HA-KODESH: lit., the Holy Tongue, i.e. the Hebrew language.
LEVIYIM: Levites, members of the tribe of Levi, who served in the Holy Temple.

MA'ASIM TOVIM: good deeds.

MERAGLIM: the scouts who were sent by Moshe Rabbeinu to spy out the Land of Israel.

MIDRASH: homiletic or non-literal interpretations of the Sages on Scripture.

MISHNAH: the codified Oral Law edited by Rabbi Yehudah Ha-Nasi; a specific paragraph of the Oral Law.

NE'EMAN: faithful.

NER CHANUKAH: a light that is lit to celebrate the Festival of Chanukah.

NESHAMAH: the soul.

NISAYON: a test or trial.

OLAM HA-BA: the World to Come.

PARASHAS HA-SHAVUA: the weekly Torah portion.

PESUKEI D'ZIMRAH: the section of the morning prayers in which we recite verses of praise on God's greatness, as a preparation for saying the *Shema* and the *Shemoneh Esreh*.

RASHA: an evil person.

RESHUS HA-RABBIM: a public domain.

RESHUS HA-YACHID: a private domain.

RIBBONO SHEL OLAM: Master of the Universe (God).

RUACH HA-KODESH: Divine inspiration.

SEFER: a book; a sacred book.

SHEMA (YISRAEL): lit. "Hear (O Israel)," the opening words of the fundamental Jewish prayer which proclaims the unity of God.

SHEMITTAH: the seventh, Sabbatical, year, in which the Torah requires a cessation of agricultural labor in Eretz Yisrael.

SHEMONEH ESREH: lit., "eighteen"; the eighteen blessings of the *Amidah* prayer.

SHULCHAN ARUCH: lit., "a prepared table"; the Code of Jewish Law, written by Rabbi Yosef Karo.

SIMAN TOV: a good (propitious) sign.

SUKKAH: a temporary dwelling in which Jews live during the Festival of Sukkos.

TAHARAH: ritual purity.

TALMID: a student; a Torah student.

TANNA'IM: Jewish scholars and teachers in the time of the Mishnah.

TERUMAH: sanctified food designated for the Kohen.

TESHUVAH: repentance.

TIKKUN: rectification.

TZADDIK: a righteous and holy person.
TZEDAKAH: charity, gifts for the poor; justice.

YERUSHALAYIM SHEL MALAH: Heavenly Jerusalem.
YERUSHALAYIM SHEL MATAH: earthly Jerusalem.
YIDDISHE NESHAMOS: (Y.) Jewish souls.
YOM TOV: lit., "a good day"; a Jewish Festival.
YOVEL: the fiftieth (Jubilee) year, following seven *shemittah* cycles.

ZIVUG: one's destined marriage partner.